Co-creating
at Its BEST

OTHER HAY HOUSE PRODUCTS BY DR. WAYNE W. DYER

BOOKS

Being in Balance
Change Your Thoughts—Change Your Life
Don't Die with Your Music Still in You (with Serena Dyer)
Everyday Wisdom
Everyday Wisdom for Success
Excuses Begone!
Getting in the Gap (book-with-audio-download)
Good-bye, Bumps! (children's book with Saje Dyer)
I Am (children's book with Kristina Tracy)
I Can See Clearly Now
Incredible You! (children's book with Kristina Tracy)
Inspiration
The Invisible Force
It's Not What You've Got! (children's book with Kristina Tracy)
Living the Wisdom of the Tao
My Greatest Teacher (with Lynn Lauber)
No Excuses! (children's book with Kristina Tracy)
The Power of Intention
The Power of Intention gift edition
A Promise Is a Promise
The Shift
Staying on the Path
10 Secrets for Success and Inner Peace
Unstoppable Me! (children's book with Kristina Tracy)
Your Ultimate Calling
Wishes Fulfilled

AUDIO/CD PROGRAMS

Advancing Your Spirit (with Marianne Williamson)
Applying the 10 Secrets for Success and Inner Peace
The Caroline Myss & Wayne Dyer Seminar
Change Your Thoughts—Change Your Life (unabridged audio book)
Change Your Thoughts Meditation
Divine Love
Dr. Wayne W. Dyer Unplugged (interviews with Lisa Garr)
Everyday Wisdom (audio book)
Excuses Begone! (available as an audio book and a lecture)
How to Get What You Really, Really, Really, Really Want
I AM Wishes Fulfilled Meditation (with James Twyman)

I Can See Clearly Now (unabridged audio book)
The Importance of Being Extraordinary (with Eckhart Tolle)
Inspiration (abridged 4-CD set)
Inspirational Thoughts
Making the Shift (6-CD set)
Making Your Thoughts Work for You (with Byron Katie)
Meditations for Manifesting
101 Ways to Transform Your Life (audio book)
The Power of Intention (abridged 4-CD set)
A Promise Is a Promise (audio book)
Secrets of Manifesting
The Secrets of the Power of Intention (6-CD set)
10 Secrets for Success and Inner Peace
There Is a Spiritual Solution to Every Problem
The Wayne Dyer Audio Collection/CD Collection
Wishes Fulfilled (unabridged audio book)

DVDS

Change Your Thoughts—Change Your Life
Excuses Begone!
Experiencing the Miraculous
I Can See Clearly Now
The Importance of Being Extraordinary (with Eckhart Tolle)
Inspiration
Modern Wisdom from the Ancient World
My Greatest Teacher (a film with bonus material featuring Wayne)
The Power of Intention
The Shift, the movie (available as a 1-DVD program
and an expanded 2-DVD set)
10 Secrets for Success and Inner Peace
There's a Spiritual Solution to Every Problem
Wishes Fulfilled

MISCELLANEOUS

The Essential Wayne Dyer Collection (comprising *The Power of
Intention, Inspiration,* and *Excuses Begone!* in a single volume)
Inner Peace Cards
The Power of Intention Cards
The Power of Intention 2015 Calendar
The Shift Box Set (includes *The Shift* DVD
and *The Shift* tradepaper book)
10 Secrets for Success and Inner Peace Cards
10 Secrets for Success and Inner Peace gift products:
Notecards, Candle, and Journal

OTHER HAY HOUSE PRODUCTS BY ESTHER AND JERRY HICKS

(The Teachings of Abraham®)

BOOKS, CALENDAR, AND CARD DECKS

Co-creating at Its BEST

A CONVERSATION
BETWEEN
MASTER TEACHERS

DR. WAYNE W. DYER
AND ESTHER HICKS

(THE TEACHINGS OF ABRAHAM®)

HAY HOUSE, INC.
Carlsbad, California • New York City
London • Sydney • Johannesburg
Vancouver • Hong Kong • New Delhi

Published and distributed in the United States by: Hay House, Inc.: www.hayhouse.com® • ***Published and distributed in Australia by:*** Hay House Australia Pty. Ltd.: www.hayhouse.com.au • ***Published and distributed in the United Kingdom by:*** Hay House UK, Ltd.: www.hayhouse.co.uk • ***Published and distributed in the Republic of South Africa by:*** Hay House SA (Pty), Ltd.: www.hayhouse.co.za • ***Distributed in Canada by:*** Raincoast Books: www.raincoast.com • ***Published in India by:*** Hay House Publishers India: www.hayhouse.co.in

Book design: Tricia Breidenthal

Cataloging-in-Publication Data is on file at the Library of Congress

Hardcover ISBN: 978-1-4019-4844-3

10 9 8 7 6 5 4 3 2 1
1st edition, December 2014

Printed in the United States of America

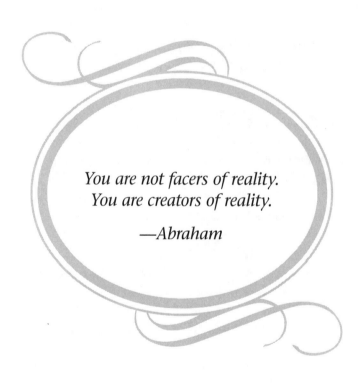

You are not facers of reality.
You are creators of reality.

—Abraham

CONTENTS

INTRODUCTION
BY DR. WAYNE W. DYER

I have carried the Teachings of Abraham with me for almost three decades now. When I was offered the opportunity to be in personal dialogue with what I have long considered to be the Leading Edge wisdom on our planet today, I immediately gave an enthusiastic response. Every time I reread this interplay between myself and the collective disembodied wisdom of Abraham, I think of the song title "Come Fly with Me." Within the pages of this book is an opportunity to soar to heights that you might never have previously imagined.

As I sat onstage talking to Esther, while listening to the amazing responses of Abraham, I was totally captivated not only by what I was hearing, but by the profound energy that was present in that large room that evening. I was like a wide-eyed little boy in a candy store who could sample anything that he desired. The teachings that are presented here in this book offer you, the reader, an opportunity to use your own mind to co-create a life that is filled with excitement, happiness, and a sense of staying on purpose at all times. Abraham responded to all of my questions and comments in the no-nonsense style that has always made me stop and contemplate the simple truths that lead to living a life in total alignment with our Source of Being.

Many years ago, as a young doctoral student I encountered the wisdom that was inherent in something called *The Strangest Secret.* Nine words put me on a path of exploring the power that lies dormant within my own mind: *You become what you think about all day long.* Here in this book, Abraham reminds me throughout the entire evening dialogue that there are no exceptions to this wondrous truth. Of all the books that I have produced and the works that I have been blessed to offer to the world, I feel that what is being given to me by Abraham in this exchange that you hold in your hands will be the most important and practical information that you will ever receive. And for those who doubt that such sagacious instruction could actually originate from the Non-Physical realm, I ask you to consider the words attributed to Mark Twain: "It ain't what you don't know that gets you into trouble; it's what you know for sure that just ain't so."

I urge you, as you read and listen to this personal meeting reproduced here in these pages, to practice a philosophy that has been a trademark for me for my entire adult life—that is, have a mind that is open to everything, and attached to nothing. The *Law of Attraction* is working right now even as you read these words, and as Abraham said to me, "the Universe doesn't hear what you say; the Universe hears how you feel."

I AM,
Wayne W. Dyer

INTRODUCTION
BY ESTHER HICKS

I knew from the very beginning of receiving Abraham that this weird but wonderful experience was happening because of the powerful desire within my husband, Jerry Hicks. His desire to be of value, to help others, to uplift, and to understand how this all works and why we are here was certainly the reason that Abraham began flowing through me. I knew that Jerry had literally summoned Abraham because of the life that he had lived and the unanswered questions that he had gathered. And so, in the beginning and for the many years that followed, the majority of Abraham's answers came in direct response to Jerry's questions. As time went by and more and more people began interacting with

Abraham, the range of questions broadened and their* message became broader and deeper.

So when Reid Tracy, president and CEO of Hay House, suggested an event where Abraham and Dr. Wayne W. Dyer could converse, I was immediately excited about it because I knew that Wayne's life had focused powerful points of understanding within him and I was very eager for him to direct any yet-unanswered questions toward Abraham. I knew it would be a powerful experience. And it was. It was co-creation at its very best!

Love,
Esther Hicks

---

* Abraham is considered a group consciousness and so is referred to in the plural.

NOTE TO READERS

This book is based on the Hay House live event that took place on November 13, 2013, in Anaheim, California, and the transcript of that event has been edited slightly in these pages in order to enhance readability. Since there aren't always physical English words to perfectly express the Non-Physical thoughts that Esther receives, she sometimes forms new combinations of words and uses standard words in new ways—for example, capitalizing them when normally they wouldn't be—in order to express new ways of looking at old ways of looking at life.

For ease of reading, the questions and comments from Dr. Wayne W. Dyer will be boldface, while the comments from Abraham will be regular typeface.

REID'S IDEA

●●●

Reid Tracy: Hello and welcome to this wonderful event. My name is Reid Tracy and I'm the president and CEO of Hay House. We are streaming this event over the Internet, so you may be a part of the show during the audience shots. There are thousands of people all over the world who will be watching along with you.

I've been at Hay House for 25 years, and this is one of the most exciting programs that I have been waiting to see myself. I called Esther up one day and I said, "I have this crazy idea. What do you think of Wayne Dyer talking to Abraham, just the two of you on the stage together?"

And she said, "I think it's a great idea."

And I said, "Oh, good. Now I'll ask Wayne."

This is going to be a super exciting evening, and so without any further ado, I'd like to welcome Wayne Dyer and Esther Hicks to the stage.

⟋⟍

Esther Hicks: Thank you very much. Hey. You guys are ready! [Esther to Reid] What have you gotten us into?

Wayne Dyer: Oh my goodness. I'm so happy to be here and talk to a ghost; I've been waiting for this for years.

Audience member: I love you, Wayne.

Wayne: Oh my goodness, I love you, too. I love all of you. It's so nice to be here.

Esther: Well, somebody asked me what we would be talking about tonight, and I said, "I don't know and I don't want to know." I didn't want to get anything in my head. But I really do like the idea of someone brilliant, like Dr. Dyer, talking to Abraham. What could be better than that? It really is co-creating at its best, isn't it?

Wayne: It really is. In 1987 or 1988 someone sent me a big collection of Abraham cassette tapes, and I started listening to them. And then Jerry and Esther and I made contact maybe a dozen years or so ago, and I've been just an incredible fan of Abraham. I think it's the wisest and most profound teachings on the planet today. I do.

Esther: Wayne has sold more of our books than we have.

Wayne: I'm a true believer. You know when someone is telling you the truth, and when you really feel the truth that's in your heart. You know you're being told exactly the way things are.

Esther: Yes. Resonance.

Wayne: Yeah, it just resonates with me. It always has. And you've never missed, in the hundreds, perhaps thousands, of times I've heard you.

Esther: I'm going to go get Abraham. Is that all right with you?

Wayne: Do you need GPS or anything like that or . . . ?

Esther: It just takes a minute for me to clear my mind and they'll say *hello,* okay? [Esther playfully to Wayne] Who are you going to go get? I have a feeling you're going to go get Abraham, too. If you really want to know, I think that's what you've been doing for a while, too.

Wayne: Well, you know, there are many times when I do exactly feel that way as well, yeah.

Esther: Okay, here I go.

WHO IS ABRAHAM?

•••

I'd first like you to just tell me and everyone watching and everyone here in this room, who you are. Who is Abraham? For those who don't know, including me. Would you tell us?

The most important thing to explain is we are a Collective Consciousness, a vibration, not different from that which all of you have access to. But because of Esther's focus over the years, she has managed to accomplish a frequency, so to speak, that allows her to hone in on us, so she can hear us in a more pointed way.

Everyone who is physically focused, and that includes all of you, is an extension of Source Energy. And we are that Source Energy that you are all extensions of. But as you move around through your day-to-day experiences, not meaning to, you often find vibrational frequencies, because of what you are observing, that prevent you from receiving the fullness of *who-you-are*. And we are the fullness of that, you see.

Some have tried to get us to define ourselves in physical terms, but we cannot. And we are not whispering words to Esther that she is repeating. We are offering blocks of thought, and Esther is finding physical words that match those blocks of thought. Everyone is capable of doing this. You all can receive this inspiration. However, you can be inspired from different points of attraction. You could be in a very bad mood and receive inspiration, but then you are not receiving inspiration from Source Energy, but instead from blocks of thought that have been left along the physical trail, so to speak.

And so it's a matter of tuning to a high frequency and doing it often enough that there is consistency to what you are receiving. That's the easiest way of explaining it. And the most important thing that we want to say to you, and to everyone, is you are all doing some of that, but you don't usually do it consistently, and Esther is not always in the mode of receiving Abraham, either. But in a forum like this, it is easy for her to receive us because of the expectation of the audience. We ride in on the momentum of the desire that all of you have already established, and then Esther translates our vibrations, our knowing, into words.

So you are really a collection of vibrations of this higher and higher frequency. Equivalent to God, would you say?

Humans have a hard time defining us, and they also have a hard time defining God. And they also have a hard time defining those who once were in physical bodies who have now reemerged back into Non-Physical.

As humans—we love you so much—you have a screwy perspective of this continuum of life. Most humans believe that you come into these bodies and you live for a little while and you get it right or you don't and then you leave, when really what is happening is you are Eternal. You never really leave.

And even when you are no longer focused in your physical bodies, you are still consciousness and you are still focused on what's going on here on Earth. There is a Collective Consciousness that is so interested, so eager about everything that you all are about. And that Source Energy is what Man wants to call God. You all have direct access to that.

So, I've often said that we're not here as human beings having a spiritual experience, but rather it's the reverse. We are infinite spiritual beings just having a temporary human experience.

When you stand in your *now* moment and you have practiced yourself into a high-flying vibration where you're not ornery, or you're not upset, or you're not worried about anything, you then allow inspiration to flow. Now, you are so much more than what you have thought yourself to be. Now, you are the extension of Source Energy. That's when you feel clarity and passion. That's when your timing is good. That's when you're at your funniest. That's when you feel the best.

You create your own reality and you do so because the thoughts that you are thinking cause you to emanate a vibrational frequency that the *Law of Attraction* is constantly responding to. And so, in all waking moments, you are creating your own point of attraction and everything that you experience is coming to you because of your vibrational emanation and the response of *Law of Attraction* to that vibration. It is as if you are standing on a sort of spinning vibrational disc and only things of the same vibration can join you on your disc. Your disc changes depending upon the thoughts that you are thinking and the emotions that you are feeling.

You choose the disc by the things that you focus on. You could choose one that feels like elation or love or freedom or joy. Or you could choose one that feels like grief or despair. You can tell what disc you are on by those who meet up with you. If you are surrounded by ornery people, you are on the ornery disc. It really is that simple. They have rendezvoused with you because you are perfect vibrational partners.

As you are able to place yourself consciously on these vibrational spinning discs, you can then understand unequivocally why every single thing that happens to you, or to anyone else, is happening.

What Is Inspiration?

• ● •

I wrote a book years ago called *Inspiration* using the two words *in-spire, in-spirito*—inspire, in spirit. And there was a great teacher on this planet a couple thousand years ago named Patanjali and he said, When you are inspired by some great purpose, some extraordinary project, all of your thoughts break their bonds. Your mind transcends limitations, your consciousness expands in every direction, and you find yourself in a new, great, wonderful world.

And then he said—and this is what I want to ask you about—when you are inspired, dormant forces, faculties, and talents come alive and you

discover yourself to be a greater person, by far, than you've ever dreamt yourself to be. It's almost as if you discover yourself to be God or Source or the Tao or Divine mind or whatever name we place on this Source Energy that you speak of and speak to us from.

The way that we have most recently been explaining that is, when you wake up in the morning, you have the potential of being in that highest frequency, because while you sleep, the momentum of your point of attraction ceases.

So when you first wake up, before you begin thinking thoughts of what went wrong yesterday or what you have to do today, you have the greatest potential of aligning with that Pure, Positive Energy.

So if you can focus there and allow a little momentum to get going, what happens is you tune in to that Source Energy consciousness who is always aware of everything you are doing. But it isn't something that just happens. You have to focus yourself into that alignment. That is the best way of describing it.

In other words, Source is there for everyone at all times. We are always there. And so when you are aware of the presence of Source and when you are not offering a vibration that prevents you from your alignment with Source, then you have those wonderful moments. And you can do that all the time. And people refer to those who are doing that as masters. But all of you can do that. It is the mastery of focus. That's what it is.

Early-Morning Momentum

• ● •

I wake up every morning at around three o'clock. Many years ago there was a great poet named Rumi, who said, "The morning breeze has secrets to tell you. Do not go back to sleep. Do not go back to sleep. Do not go back to sleep."

I've written many of the books that I have written when I've been awakened like that. What is it? What is it that awakens me? It's like I can almost tell you the exact time.

In a film I did years ago, called *The Shift*, they show a clock and it is 3:13 A.M., almost to the second, every single time. Is that the angels? Is that

Divine Source? Is that someone saying, "This is your purpose; this is the time when there are no distractions"?

The thing we most want to say is that Source is available to you at all times. But what is important about your story is that for some reason that is the time that you decide to listen.

But there's nobody else around to distract me.

And that's the important conversation to have. So what is it about that time? What is it that's happening that makes you more resonant, more receptive? It is that the momentum of your thought has stopped while you are sleeping so there is no contradictory vibration going on within you. So now you are more likely to hear.

Esther has been saying to herself when she awakens in those early-morning hours, "Am I awake? Because if I am awake, I am going to get up." In other words, she can more easily pick up on the thoughts we are offering because of the absence of resistance at that time. That's what you're talking about.

Yes. But I find for me, the most creative moments are during that middle of the nighttime.

Well, think about why that is. When you think a thought for as little as 17 seconds, *Law of Attraction* will bring another thought like it to it. So momentum ensues.

What do you mean? *Law of Attraction* **will bring another thought like it to it? What is** *Law of Attraction***?**

Let's say that you wake up in the morning, and rather than finding that clear space that is potentially there for you, instead you begin thinking about the trouble that you had yesterday at work. You remember the dilemma you were in the middle of. You think about the discomfort. You think about the discord. And as you focus for as little as 17 seconds upon that, more thoughts like those come into your mind.

If you continue to think those thoughts for another 17 seconds, there will be more momentum still. Another 17 seconds, more momentum still, until you cross something as brief as the 68-second threshold. In just that short amount of time you have missed your window of resonance with Source.

That happened to Esther recently and so we said to her, "Well, you can always begin again tomorrow with more positive thoughts." And Esther said, "I refuse to accept that I have to wait all the way until tomorrow to get back on my high-flying disc. I know I can do it by focusing."

And we agree that with some deliberate focus Esther could return to a stream of more-positive thoughts, but it is much easier to do it before negative momentum begins than after negative momentum has begun.

So we like to talk about *Law of Attraction* because it is the vibrational engine that manages everything. And we can't talk about *Law of Attraction* without talking about momentum, because there is a momentum in thought. And if you think a thought long enough, it becomes a strong habit of thought. That is what a belief is. A belief is just a thought you continue to think.

Sometimes you continue to perpetuate beliefs that do not serve you, but when you first awaken, those beliefs are inactive enough that you could find a fresh one. A fresh one that comes from Source that is about *who-you-really-are* and what you really know.

Is the reverse of that if you awaken and you have a very positive thought, such as, *I'm going to heal myself of this* . . . ?

Well, that is a wonderful thing, once you get that momentum going.

But would the 17-second rule apply to that as well?

The 17-second rule applies to everything. It is very helpful for you to acknowledge that *Law of Attraction*—whether you are aware of it or not— is responding to the vibration that you are offering right now, and therefore momentum is occurring. So, if we were standing in your physical shoes and the thought felt good, we would focus on it. We would think more about it. We would talk about it. We would write it down. We would discuss it with others. We would deliberately encourage that momentum. But if it is an uneasy thought that feels uncomfortable, then we would do our best to generalize it.

The more specific you are in a thought, the faster the momentum. The more general you are in a thought, the slower the momentum.

Esther remembers being in San Francisco and driving to the top of one of those hills. She couldn't believe that people were actually driving up and down them. So imagine perching your car at the top of one of those hills and taking it out of gear and taking the parking brake off. And now, just for fun to see what will happen, you nudge your car a little bit from behind. Well, you know what will happen. With only a slight nudge your car will careen down the hill.

But if you step out in front of it right away and let it bump up against you, you can easily stop that unwanted momentum. You would not want to be at the base of that hill trying to stop the momentum.

And so your thoughts are the same way. Every thought is vibration, and *Law of Attraction* is responding to every thought, and therefore the thought is going to increase. The only question is: Is this thought one that you want to increase? Because it is going to increase. *Law of Attraction* insists that it will.

WHAT ABOUT
AFFIRMATIONS?

• ● •

I talk a lot about the *"I AM" Discourses.* "*I AM*" is another name for Source. If you are feeling weak but you have a thought saying, *I am strong,* or *I am well,* or *I am healed,* or *I am wealthy,* or *I am positive,* or *I am loving* . . . I mean that's one of the lines from the book of Joel. "Let the weak man say, I am strong."

It makes sense; however, there is an effort factor that can have a backfiring effect, because every subject is really two subjects: wanted and absence of wanted. So, if you are feeling not strong but you say,

"I am strong," which end of the stick are you actually activating?

When you feel the need to apply strong effort, you are usually trying to overcome what you have actually got going on vibrationally. And so, instead of it working out the way you want it to, it works in reverse. In other words, you are trying to make those affirmations and actions compensate for vibration that is going in opposition to what you really want. And your words cannot buck that current. That's why you feel the need to try harder.

Affirmations are wonderful, but we would make sure that we are feeling really good when we affirm, because the Universe does not hear what you say; the Universe hears what you mean.

It also responds to how you feel, doesn't it?

That's right. That's how you know what you mean. So, if you're feeling weak but you are proclaiming that you're strong, the louder you shout it the more the Universe is hearing you demanding something that you do not feel, or believe, which is the reason that you are trying so hard.

It is as if you go down to the edge of the river with your canoe and you put it in the water and you point it upstream and then you paddle very hard, because you believe that in order to get something done there should be some struggle involved. But *Law of Attraction* is providing the path of least resistance.

You are Source Energy, and there is a trajectory of ease. It is a path of least resistance, and you can feel when you're on that trajectory, and you can feel when you get off it. The more you proclaim that you are on it, the more you are often off it and trying to get on it. Sometimes it is better just to take a nap.

CHOICES BEFORE COMING FORTH

• ● •

All right. I've got a very important question. Not that these haven't been. I have eight children.

[Playfully] You have our condolences.

Well, before I had any children, I had eight theories about how to raise children. And now I have eight children and no theories about how to raise children. I have a daughter; her name is Serena. And when she was about nine or ten years old, she used to always complain to me about my fathering, about my parenting, you know, giving me lots of advice about how I do this wrong and that wrong.

And I had been listening to some of the things that Abraham was saying and then one day I just got fed up with her complaining and I said to her, "You know, if you don't like the kind of father that I am, the kind of parent that I am, then you shouldn't be blaming me. You should really be taking a look at yourself and asking yourself why in the world you would pick me to be your father."

And she put her hands on her hips, rolled her eyes at me—you know, that ten-year-old kind of look—and she said, "You're telling me that I actually picked you to be my father and picked Mom to be my mother?"

I said, "Exactly right. And when you're making important decisions like that, you should really be very careful about them."

Also, "You are right now evoking the kind of parent I am being. Your expectation is so powerful, I cannot override it. We seem to have rendezvoused on a vibrational spot that makes each of us want to blame the other for what's going on here."

So her final response to me, which was the best response I think I've ever heard from one of my kids, was "Well, then, I must have been in a hurry."

And so my question to you, Abraham, is: Do we have access to knowing or choosing who our parents are going to be before we show up in this world of form?

Yes.

How does that work?

Well, there is a powerful trajectory. It is a powerful, but general, plan. You knew that you were coming forth, and you knew that the variety would be perfect. You knew that the variety would inspire you to your personal new preferences.

But when you say you knew, in what way? I mean, there's no brain to work with, there's no body to work with. You're in this formless—

[Playfully] What does brain have to do with Consciousness and knowing?

You're the one who has to answer that.

The brain is the focusing mechanism that you are utilizing here. But there is Consciousness that is outside of what you call the human focus of the brain. That's this vibrational thing we continually talk about. We talk about vibration. We talk about Energy. We talk about thought. And eventually, once enough momentum has occurred, you will feel emotion. We want to acknowledge that the emotions that you feel are manifestations. And there is a significant amount of momentum that has occurred before your emotions show you how well aligned, or not, you are with that Broader Perspective.

So, before you came into this physical body, you were Consciousness. And you were eager about projecting some of that Consciousness into a physical body, because you knew that in this physical body, with all of the other wonderful and diverse physical beings that would share this time-space reality with you, that you would be inspired to new ideas. And that really turned you on, because you are an Eternal Being. And you knew that being born into a physical body, surrounded by the variety and contrast of planet Earth, that you would be stimulated to new ideas and that without new ideas that Eternity would cease. But of course, you knew that Eternity will not cease. You knew that this time-space reality would continue to inspire the new ideas. So you had a general sense of your Well-Being, and you understood your absolute worthiness.

One of the great benefits, for Esther and for all of you, because of Jerry making his transition in Non-Physical is that Esther now has a keen sense of his continuing existence and of his awareness and interest in the things that she is now doing. She can feel his Consciousness, and she can feel her alignment with him. She can feel when she is off on a path that he is not a Vibrational Match to. And Jerry, you see, is an example of the Non-Physical Consciousness that has always been there.

Humans often believe that the continuum of life is about one generation being born and then another and then another, but that is not the true continuum of life. The true continuum of life is that you come forth into a physical body; you explore contrast and variety and you find things that interest you and delight you, that amaze you and that encourage you; and you continually give birth to new desires. And those things that interest you, those desires that you give birth to, do not stop when you make your transition back into Non-Physical. Instead you join that cadre of Non-Physical Consciousness who is keenly interested in the things that you were interested in before you experienced what humans call death. But now, from your Non-Physical perspective, you are interested from a place of no resistance. You no longer contradict your desires with doubt and unworthiness. Now you are Pure, Positive Energy, you see.

The thrill bumps that you experience are evidence of our enthusiasm for what you are experiencing in that moment. You think those thrill bumps belong only to you, but they are actually you resonating with the way we feel. So never confuse the fact that we are Non-Physically focused, and therefore formless, with being mindless or emotionless or disinterested.

INTERACTING WITH THOSE "PASSED"

I know that in a timeless world there is no before and after. And like you just said, Jerry just left the physical world, and my mom just left the physical world a short time ago. Is she capable of recognizing me?

Not only capable of recognizing you but doing it all day, every day. But you have to reorient yourself about your mother, because when she reemerged into Non-Physical, she left behind all doubt and fear and worry and all of those personality characteristics that she picked up along her physical trail.

That is why we like to remind you that when you wake up in the morning you have the potential of pushing the reset button, because that is what happens when you reemerge back into Non-Physical. You push the reset button. You do not lose interest. In fact, your interest is keener than ever before. But you cannot find resonance with her if you are remembering her as she was while still in her body, before she left all of her resistance behind.

I was in Glasgow, Scotland, this summer, and it was just a short time after my mother passed away. And she was there in the room with me.

Yes. She is watching for moments when you are not offering resistance.

After she passed, for the first time I had a sort of a waking dream, a lucid dream. She died at 96, but she was in her 40s in my dream. I drove up the driveway and I went to open the door, but there was a screen door there that had never been there, and I couldn't get the screen door open.

Because the screen door represented the resistance that you're accustomed to seeing.

And then my mother just opened the door. She opened it inward, by the way. She opened it inward. And I said to her, "You can't be here. You can't be here; you're dead, you're dead." And as I said those words, she faded away.

Because your ability to see her changed.

And she became old, old. Her arms went from a 40-year-old woman's arms to a 96-year-old woman's arms.

Yes, well, she would like you to cut that out.

I talked to Louise Hay—a dear friend of mine and Esther—and she said the reason that my mother couldn't stay there with me—

It is not that she couldn't stay, but that you couldn't see her. You see, it was your human inability to perceive, not the absence of her.

So the concept of death—

There is no death.

Right.

There's only life and more life. And now, the concept of death equals clarity and eagerness and fun and fullness and sureness and certainty and worthiness and passion and interest in what you are about. More so than ever before! While in her physical body she was never able to understand the true magnificence of that which you are. But now she does. She had no idea how good you are. She loved you, but not like she does now.

I feel her now.

Yes, she's all over the place, isn't she? [Abraham looks to the audience and asks] Do you see auras floating around here? Yes.

HE FORGAVE HIS FATHER

Since I've got the microphone and I get to talk to you, I'd like to talk about my own experience as a young boy. I spent the first ten years of my life in a series of foster homes, and orphanages and so on.

My father was a man who just walked away. He spent some time in jail. He was a very abusive man. He left my mother with three boys under the age of four. He just disappeared. Long story . . .

Just the way you planned it. It was the trajectory you wanted, because you are a freedom seeker to the core of your being and you didn't want anybody bossing you around.

Yes, I've heard my kids say that many, many times, and I've often said that when a little kid says, "You're not the boss of me," that is not a bratty little kid; that's someone saying, "I have to be free."

They are saying, "I'm autonomous. I've come with great reason. I have Guidance from Source. I'll tune in to who I AM."

So, I never met my father. And I grew up with rage in my heart toward this man who could walk away and just never look back, and never pay any support, and never even ask a question about his three boys or anything. I was the youngest.

He did his part. He gave you an avenue into physical. Most parents mess it up far more than that.

Did I choose him to be my father?

Yes. Deliberately.

Because the most significant moment in my life was in 1974 when I was 34 years old, and I was at his grave in Biloxi, Mississippi. And before that I was drinking and I was overweight and my life was out of control. I was not taking good care of myself. I was writing. I'd written some textbooks. But the kind of writing I really wanted to do, I just couldn't get it. It just wouldn't come.

You were too angry.

Yeah, I was filled with rage. I would wake up in dreams, on almost a nightly occurrence, and I'd just be screaming and I'd be fighting him and I'd be sweating.

I went to his grave—it was the 30th of August, 1974—and I really went there to do something on his grave. I was there for two hours or so, and I went back to the car to drive back to New Orleans and then back to New York—I was teaching; I was a professor at St. John's University in New York—but something called me back.

How far down the road did you get before you were called back?

I only got to the car. I was in the car and something said, "Go back to the grave." And I went back to his grave, and I was sobbing and I forgave my father. I said, "From this moment on, I send you love." And I did a film about him, and I called him my greatest teacher.

Everything in my life changed and turned around. My writing took off. I wrote a book that became an international bestseller. It all came when I released that rage and anger . . .

What do you think happened? Because he was always there with you. He was always loving you. He was always proud of you. He was always appreciating you.

Really?

Because he's Source Energy. So that's how he was feeling—

Even while he was here on this planet?

Oh, no. He was all pinched off then.

Yeah, he was in jail a big part of that.

But once he reemerged into Non-Physical, he was in that place of Pure, Positive Energy. And his influence was therefore strong. And your desire to understand all of this; your desire to teach this; your desire to let go of the resistance that was holding you back was also strong. In other words, when you forgive someone, you let go of the resistance that is keeping you from your alignment.

And it really doesn't have anything to do with the actual subject that you are angry about. But it feels like it does, because that's what you're focused upon. So we are asking you: What do you think happened? You went there with strong desire. Can you articulate that?

Yes. I can articulate to the point of saying I went there because I wanted to see his death certificate. I wanted to know if he even acknowledged that he had a son named Wayne. I just wanted to know that.

So your bitterness was still very strong.

But there was something that was driving me. My other two brothers couldn't care less about it, at all. And our mother would never talk to me about it. She just said he was an asshole. My

mother never used language like that except that one time.

What was driving you was the trajectory of Well-Being. What was driving you was the understanding that you weren't born to be dependent on someone else. And you did not come to use someone else as your excuse for not being in alignment.

And so something happened in that moment that caused you to let go of that. Maybe it just got old. Maybe it just felt futile. Maybe you felt the ridiculousness of it. Maybe it had just gone on too long. Or maybe there was a reset button. Maybe you had found a desire that was stronger than your old beliefs, and for just a moment the desire took precedence. The desire that is coming forth from within.

We've written a handful of books, and in every book there are processes, and every process is written to help you to find a way to release resistance. Some processes help you to go right to the resistant point; however, if you hit that point of resistance too head-on, it can sometimes make the resistance worse, because with that habit of thought, or belief, there is momentum.

So something happened to you that caused you to cease the resistant momentum that you had going for so long, and to feel, for a moment, the fullness of *who-you-really-are*. What you felt was the powerful God Force love that was pouring through your father, your Non-Physical father, focused upon you, wanting you to feel it.

The best way for us to say it is that his love was stronger than your hate. And he caught you at a weak moment when your hatred was less focused. And you felt it. There is no greater message that we wish to convey. That is what we are talking about all day, every day.

People ask about healing. They want to find someone who can help them. And we say, you know, Source is flooding this Energy of Well-Being toward you at all times. You don't need any other to do what Source is already doing. But if someone can help you to soften your resistance so that you can somehow be receptive to the love and Well-Being that's being flowed, a little bit of alignment goes a long way. And as you say, it is life-changing. Your life turned on a dime, because you returned to the path of least resistance—to the lover that you are. And you took big steps in leaving that hatred behind.

Is there only love on the other side?

Yes.

There's only love.

Yes. Only love. Only love. Only, only, only, only Pure, Positive Energy, love and clarity and passion and eagerness. Yes.

Contrast and Your Point of Attraction

Sometimes in my talks, I speak about this whole idea of transcending the duality, like this physical world is all duality. It's up/down, good/bad, male/female, east/west . . .

That helps you to focus. In other words, if you don't know what you don't want, you cannot know what you do want. We call that Step One in the creative process. The contrast, or what you are calling duality, causes you to ask. But humans often make such a lifestyle out of staying in that back-and-forth, up-and-down mode of asking that they keep themselves vibrationally confused. You do want the contrast to help you to ask, but you do not want to make your life only about the asking, Step One mode.

So when I step out of this, when I take my last breath and step out into the Non-Physical, will there be no opposites?

There is contrast in the Non-Physical, but from your physical perspective, it will be so slight by comparison to the resistance that you are accustomed to that it is indiscernible.

What do you mean by *contrast*?

Variety, difference. Knowing what you don't want and therefore knowing what you do want. So that causes you to launch vibrational rockets of desire, so to speak.

There are three steps to the process of creation. The first step is to ask, and contrast helps you to pinpoint that. Step Two happens when Source receives those vibrational requests and immediately becomes a Vibrational Match to them. That is why we say, "When you ask, it is immediately given."

But there's often quite a vibrational gap between what people are asking for and where they are usually hanging around vibrationally. That's what you were talking about earlier. You were asking for a feeling of forgiveness, but you were hanging around in something that felt quite different. And it is that *vibrational gap* that is the reason for any discomfort.

So then, Step Three is what we've been calling *allowing*. That's where you find some way to find vibrational alignment with what you're asking for. In the larger scheme of things, it really is the path of least resistance, but if you've been practicing thoughts that feel like hatred or fear, then it often doesn't feel like the path of least resistance, because it is not easy to find. That is why you ultimately re-emerge back into Non-Physical.

When you are able to close that vibrational gap between what you're asking for and what Source has already answered so that your vibration in the moment is in the same vibrational place as your desire, then you can receive the inspiration. Then you can begin to realize the details of what you've been asking for.

We have been talking a lot recently about your *point of attraction*. Most people have no idea that they are emanating a signal, and that everything that comes to them is coming in response to the signal that they are emitting. We call that your *point of attraction*.

Your emotions are clear indicators of the vibrational mix you have going on at any point in time between your desire about a subject and the beliefs that you hold about the same subject. You have an *Emotional Guidance System* that is composed of all the emotions that you feel from fear and despair, to better-feeling emotions such as frustration and overwhelment, to even-better-feeling emotions such as hope and love and joy and appreciation. The better feeling the emotion, the less vibrational variance between your current active thought and your desire.

When you feel an emotion, such as orneriness, it is as if you are on a spinning ornery disc of attraction, which makes it likely that you will be rendez-vousing with other ornery people as long as that is the spinning disc that you are on. In other words, when you are having a day where you are meeting many people who are ornery, it would be good for you to realize that you are on the ornery disc. That is your point of attraction and that is why they are coming to you. Esther says it's like the seven dwarfs. There's the Ornery disc and the Happy disc, and the Grumpy disc. She's got about 200 dwarfs now. Passive-Aggressive disc . . .

It can be very helpful to understand that you do have a point of attraction and that you can control it. And your best opportunity to control it is when you first awaken each morning. It doesn't take long to transform your point of attraction; 20 or 30 or 40 or 50 days of waking up in nonresistance and then deliberately focusing to maintain your state of lesser and lesser resistance will make a big difference in how you feel and the things that come into your experience. You will begin to receive insight and positive manifestations such as good-feeling emotions and good ideas will begin to flow to you.

As Esther began to experience that consciously and began to personally see the benefit of her morning focus, she said, "Please call it Step Four!" Because when you hang around on that high-flying disc consistently and make it all the way through breakfast without falling off and then all the way until lunchtime and then all the way through the day, you are then able to recognize the association between the lovely things that are happening to you in this day and the resistance-free vibration that you have deliberately accomplished. And then, and only then, are you able to consciously co-create with Non-Physical. So now we are getting right to the heart of the question that you just asked about the existence of contrast in the Non-Physical. It is such a good question.

So see yourself on this high-flying disc, feeling really good. You've been there for a while, and there is evidence happening in your life experience that confirms that you are there. You are rendezvousing with nice people; traffic is nicer to you; you're finding good parking places; and most of all, you feel clarity! You feel no confusion. Things are working out in your life experience on all fronts. And you can tell that you have shifted, like you said. You have made a dramatic vibrational shift. And now it is sustainable, because you did it on purpose. You practiced it and now you own it. It is yours.

But now, even from that vibrational place of supreme alignment, still problems can present themselves to you. There is still contrast. But the difference is now the problem doesn't rip you from the disc. Instead it looks like an opportunity; like something that's interesting; like something that you'd like to think about. It doesn't look like something that overwhelms you or overtakes you or defeats you. Now contrast is simply options or choices.

It is a lovely thing to understand that you are vibrational and then to offer your vibration on purpose and to watch how everything responds to the vibration that you are purposefully offering. And then to be awakened at poignant moments like at 3:13 in the morning.

Can we reach that state of love that has no opposite, joy that has no opposite, while we're still here in physical?

You wouldn't want to do that, for this reason: If contrast were to cease, expansion would also cease. And expansion is necessary for eternity. In other words, without choices, there could not be more. And without more, then we would all cease to be.

There Is So Much Violence

———— • ● • ————

There is so much violence on our planet. And there was violence in my heart when I went to Biloxi to find my father.

But there is a big difference between a consistent state of feeling anger and the emotion of despair. There is a big difference between the emotion of revenge and the emotion of love or joy or appreciation.

We would far rather see you feeling revenge than despair. We would rather you feel revenge than guilt. And we would rather that you feel overwhelment rather than rage, and hope rather than overwhelment, and love rather than hope.

In other words, there can always be an improvement in your vibration, and that really is what we are all about. Source continues to find higher and higher, purer and purer vibrations because of the contrast that you are sifting your way through.

Humans have the misconception that Source is no longer expanding or that Source is finished and perfect, and that humans are now working to accomplish that perfection. But what is really going on is that Source is expanding into greater capacities of love because of that which Man is living.

When large segments of your population are in abject hatred, you are launching rockets of desire that take Source to new heights. In other words, the love in the Non-Physical becomes greater because of the hate that you are living. That is the expansion that we're talking about.

But no value is realized by you if you don't then line up with the newly created desire. Once that rocket has been launched and the new desire exists, Source never returns to the lower vibration again. And so in order for your alignment to take place, you have to reach for the higher vibration and accomplish it. That is what we mean by being on the high-flying disc.

Sometimes Esther playfully tells us, "Abraham, I'm not in such a good mood, and I think you should lower your vibration to blend with me, because I know that this negative emotion that I'm feeling is because you are vibrationally up there and I am vibrationally down here. So if you would come down where I am, then I wouldn't feel the separation." And we tell her, "We're not coming down. You've got to come up."

But doesn't all of humanity have to come up?

Yes. And you all do when you make your transition back into Non-Physical in what you call your death experience. But we don't think you should have to croak to be happy. We know that you can practice yourselves into vibrational alignment with the Source within you.

CAN A HANDFUL IMPACT MILLIONS?

●◉●

But can one of us, or two of us, or a handful of us who are living close to this Source Energy, from a place of Divine love . . . can we impact millions of people?

You can, because one who's connected to this Energy is more powerful than millions who are not. But it is important to understand that your mother was in that pure, high vibration and yet she could not get your attention. In other words, she is Pure, Positive Energy, focused on you all day every day, but you had to be in the right frequency in order to hear her.

And so that's the way it is with Source. Source is in that high frequency, but you've got to be in the vibrational vicinity in order to feel it. And until you've felt it, you can't know it. You can't get it from our words. No one can get it from your words. Nothing can replace the experience of the releasing of resistance, like what happened to you at that grave site that day. There just aren't enough words in the world to explain what happened.

Right on.

As you released your resistance, you aligned with Source Energy, and with your father, in that moment, you see.

It's been my teaching mission to help others understand that. I mean, it was an act of forgiveness, if you will, that totally transformed my entire life and affected millions and millions of people.

[Playfully] But what took you so long to get there? In other words, everyone would feel better if they would just think thoughts that feel better. But it is as Esther said to us often in the beginning: "But, Abraham, it is true. This unwanted thing actually did happen. Therefore, shouldn't I think about it?"

And we explained to her that there are many things that are true that feel good when you focus upon them and there are many things that are true that feel horrible when you focus upon them. We would be selective about what we focus upon because when you focus upon the things that feel horrible, you're out there on the raw and ragged edge, seemingly without your Source. Of course, you are never really without your Source because Source never stops perceiving life through you, but sometimes you hold a vibrational frequency that causes you to be resistant to the vibration of Source so it feels like you are pinched off. And then you miss so many realizations and there is so much that you do not recognize.

Can't someone who's living closer to Source Energy have an impact in a family or in a community?

Yes, certainly.

Isn't that what Abraham is doing?

Certainly. But people have to be ready. They have to be in the vibrational vicinity. You cannot set your radio dial on 98 and hear what's being broadcast on 101. The frequencies have to match up. Too often people beat up on themselves when things aren't going well. They become self-derogatory. And we want them to understand there is always a vibrational choice that they do have some control over if they will try a little bit. That's why we are so emphatic about your early-morning thoughts. Find some general thought that feels good and try to stay there until some of the momentum gets going, and then notice how this day is different because you did that. And after 30 days of doing that, you'll know what we're talking about.

Programming
Before Sleep

• • •

What about the last five minutes before you go to sleep? I often tell people that when you are in slumber, your subconscious mind starts to get programmed. And if five minutes before you are going off to sleep you are thinking about all the things that went wrong and how this isn't happening and this is never going to work and I'm struggling financially and I'm sick, aren't you programming your subconscious mind? And you wake up and the Universe then offers you the experiences that match up to what you've placed in there.

Yes, we agree with you.

So those last five minutes, it seems to me, it's like you want to put in there all of your I-am's. I am content. I am—

But here's the thing. If you've had a hard day, you can't just say it different in the last five minutes, because the Universe doesn't hear what you say; the Universe hears how you feel. So your best chance of really feeling good is after a night of momentum slowing rather than after a day of momentum increasing.

That's very well-said.

Yes. Certainly, it is always better to speak positively. But don't you find yourself sometimes challenging your own thoughts? People sometimes feel as if their thoughts are thinking them rather than the other way around. If you have a negative train of thought going, make it more general if you can. Step back from the specifics of it.

I'm just thinking, you're going to sleep for eight hours, let's say, and you're going to marinate

**in whatever thoughts that you have just filled
your subconscious mind with.**

Not really. That is the thing that we are really
wanting to explain. *Law of Attraction,* and the momentum of *Law of Attraction,* is not active while you
are unconscious. Now, it is logical that when you
wake up, you will refocus and that your habit of
thought, your beliefs, your propensity of thoughts
will pick up where you left off . . . but that can
change with this new understanding about getting a
different trajectory going.

Someone the other day gave us an excellent word
because he has been deliberately waking up in a
higher-feeling vibration and managing to maintain
it throughout the day with some consistent success.
He said he is on his 60th or 70th day of that. He told
us, "Now it's beginning to feel like I'm *tethered* there.
Sometimes I do dip down, but it's like a bungee cord
that takes me right back up."

And we said, "That's exactly what we're saying
about this Non-Physical You." You are tethered.
You are tethered to this Pure, Positive Energy. But
you've practiced not being in the pure high frequency enough that you've sort of stretched your bungee cord out to its limits. And now you're dangling
around in vibrations that don't serve you and that

are not really *who-you-are.* But it doesn't take much to get that elasticity back.

Is this like a conditioning process? I mean, like from the time that we're little boys and we're little girls, we're told what we can do, what we can't do, what's possible, what's not possible.

Yes, by those who don't know. By those who are looking from lower discs, who are wanting to prepare you for the inevitable failure that they think you will live. And in the early days, you didn't like that at all. You protested in the beginning. The Source within you knows *who-you-are,* and is always reminding you of that. That's why you experienced, sometimes in the middle of your sleep at 3:13, some of those thoughts.

PARENT-CHILD DYNAMICS

---•●•---

There's a poet, William Wordsworth, who said, "Our birth is but a sleep and a forgetting .... Heaven lies about us in our infancy."

It is a forgetting in the sense that you don't remember the details. But you remember your worthiness. You know your value. You know you came with purpose. That's why when people try to tell you otherwise, you don't take it well, in the beginning. Over time they can condition you to let go of remembering that, but you can spring back. Start tomorrow morning.

Yeah. But I'm thinking about all the parents out there. And how often they do condition their children with "You can't do this," or "That's not possible," or—

If we were giving one encouragement to parents, it would be to deliberately choose your emotional disc—your alignment with *who-you-really-are*—and then talk to your kids. Don't let the subject at hand be the reason for choosing your emotional disc. Don't let the fact that they have misbehaved or disobeyed be the reason that you feel the way you do.

Observing unwanted things causes you to choose the unwanted emotional disc. Some have lifetimes of hating because of that. But you could choose what you focus upon because you want to feel good, and then words that are inspired will follow that. Remember that others have *Inner Beings,* too.

Your *Inner Being* knows everything that you've asked for. It's swirling in this vibrational reality. Your *Inner Being* knows everything that you want and where you are right now in relationship to everything that you want. And your *Inner Being* knows the path of least resistance to get you to your desire, you see. So when you begin practicing what the path of least resistance feels like, then you can guide some others, too.

Couldn't we get it from babies? I mean, couldn't we learn from babies?

Yes, hang around with them. They know it.

Yeah. I've been hanging around quite a good amount of time lately with a little boy named Jessie. He's two years old, and—

You can feel his wisdom.

Oh my goodness.

His knowing, his love.

I'm just so in love with this little boy. When I take him by myself down to the swimming pool and I'm just with him, I look him in the eye, I just ask him about God. I ask him about Source Energy. I say, "Tell me more."

And what he says is "You make too much of all of this." And "Don't make me think about things that I don't want to think about yet." And "I'm new here and I really like it so far." And "I want everybody to feel about it like I feel about it." And "I would like to maintain this alignment with my Source Energy through all the days of my life experience." And "It's fun to hang out with somebody like you, who has reconnected with all of that. And so you feel really good to me. You don't feel like most people. You feel like that which I know to be. That's why I gravitate to you." That's what he's saying.

It's amazing, Abraham, because the first time I saw him—he was five or six months old—I recognized him. It wasn't only that he is a cute little boy. I saw myself in him as a little baby myself.

You felt resonance with his alignment. In other words, he's tuned in, tapped in, turned on. He hasn't disconnected from that. He's still tethered, you see.

He just brings so much joy, even thinking about him, and his little face, and about making him laugh.

The infusion of new ones coming into the world brings great value to the world. You think that you are here to teach them, but actually they are coming to teach you. They are teaching you—animals are teaching you, too—about the high-flying disc. They are saying to you, "Don't mess it up."

And we do mess it up.

You don't mean to. And you don't have to, and when you do, you do not feel good. Whenever you deviate from the vibration of *who-you-are,* you feel the pinching off. And you feel relief when you no longer pinch it off. If you want to practice no longer pinching off your Connection to Source, take some subject that you feel resistance about and just become more general about it—and notice what happens.

What do you mean?

For example. Let's go back in time before you had that wonderful realignment with *who-you-really-are* at the grave site, to the time when you were still railing about the inappropriateness of your ne'er-do-well father. It's eating you up. You feel the discord in a very strong way. You don't want to feel the discord, but you can't change what happened. You can't change the stories that you have heard about him, and you can't seem to change the way you feel about it. It's a strong momentum within you and you don't like the way it feels.

You could change the subject and think about things that feel better, but with something as significant as a parent-and-child relationship, it comes up often. There are so many reminders around as you see parents with their kids. So, even though it is important for you to find a way of soothing the resistance, instead you say things such as "I can't believe how that guy just left us. I can't believe how he turned his back on us." And with those kinds of thoughts, the negative momentum gets stronger.

"He never even looked back. I don't think he even acknowledged that I was alive. I don't think he cared about me at all. He certainly didn't care about the others. He didn't care about my mother." Now the negative momentum is picking up more speed.

The more thoughts like that you think, the faster the momentum and the worse you feel. You can get enough strong negative momentum going that you can hold yourself out of alignment with *who-you-really-are* for a long time.

But now let's say you are aware that you do not want to do that. Maybe you have listened to someone like us. And so you say to yourself, "I just want to feel better about this. And I really don't know what my father was thinking. I don't know what was going on in his world. Nobody's really explained to me how he felt. He may have felt broken. He may not have felt like he had anything to offer any of us. He may have felt like we were better off without him.

I don't know what he really felt. I do know that he provided an avenue for me into this time-space reality. I'm glad about that. And I do know that I had a lot of contrast early on, and I think that has served me. And I do know that the relief I will feel when I let go of this is going to be pretty significant. And I don't believe that Source hates him."

I agree.

"I don't believe that Source is focused upon what's wrong with him. Oh, maybe that's why I feel so awful. Because I have a differing opinion with Source about my father."

And when I step out of this form?

You'll reemerge into the opinion that Source has about everything.

And what about my father? Will he be there?

Right there. Oh, right there, right there. And offering no explanation whatsoever. Don't look for closure; there is no closure. It just keeps opening. You never get to the bottom of anything. *Law of Attraction* just gives you more detail.

Did I need to have all of that contrast, all of that rage, in order to get to—

You didn't need it, but you didn't not want it. You said, "I'll go forth. I'll figure it out. I'm a teacher, and I'm going to teach a lot of people. And the majority of people aren't born into feathered nests or onto high-flying discs. And I'm a teacher. I want to write books that will assist them. And I can't write what I don't know."

HE CAN SEE
CLEARLY NOW

• ● •

Ah. You can't imagine what you just touched in me, because I've just written a book called *I Can See Clearly Now.*

Clarity is Esther's new favorite word, because when you're on that high-flying disc, clarity feels better than anything. It feels wonderful to be clear-minded, which means to be sure-footed and know what to do. The book is *I Can See Clearly Now*?

I Can See Clearly Now. It's also a song . . .

"I am remembering everything that I knew before I came forth into this physical body, and so much more that I picked up along my physical trail. All of the contrast that I have lived has put things into my Vortex that for a long time I didn't allow myself to see. But now I'm a Vibrational Match to everything that I've put there, and it's a beautiful world that I have created.

"I've put enough in my Vortex to keep myself busy for 20 or 30 lifetimes, and I'm eager about all of that. I see where the world is going. I see that others have the capacity to do this, too. I see that no one needs to hold themselves in a state of discomfort or disconnection. There's no reason for that. I see that Source is right here for all of us, whispering to us, speaking clearly to us. All we have to do is just listen a little."

That's what I was going to ask you, because what I've done with this book is I've written 58 chapters and each one of them is . . . I'm going along this way and then suddenly I'm making a left turn or a right turn or I'm doing an about-face. You know, like the first five books that I wrote for the public, I never mentioned the words *spirit*, *God*, *consciousness*. Higher consciousness

was never mentioned. I wrote books about psychology, etc.

Your readers weren't ready.

But then I wrote a book called *You'll See It When You Believe It*. And in looking back at the index, that book contained, like, 39 references to those things. And then the next book has it in the title. And then I'm giving lectures about it.

Is there some force? I mean, I made a dramatic shift one time on the Long Island Expressway. I was teaching at the university in 1976, shortly after the visit to my father's grave, and I was driving down the LIE, which means *lie,* and I pulled off to the side. It was something overwhelming. I was about to be granted tenure at this university. Everybody was looking for tenure and wanted tenure. Tenure means you've got a job here for the rest of your life. You're guaranteed to be staying right here in this office, doing the same thing that you've been doing for the last six years.

But it was like a frightening kind of feeling for me. How do you turn down tenure? I mean, it was hard to get . . . I was going to be a full professor. I was going to have a guaranteed job!

And I pulled off, and something just was overwhelming. I mean, I actually got flushed, and I got back in the car. I didn't call my family. I drove right to the university, went into the dean's office—her name was Sarah Fasenmyer—and I said, "Dr. Fasenmyer, this is my last semester." I'd written a book called *Your Erroneous Zones.* I just took it out and I said, "I can't take this."

I wrote about that in the book *I Can See Clearly Now.* That powerful moment when I knew. Was that Source Energy? What was that? And from that moment on, I gave up all the benefits that you get from being employed.

You gave up bondage.

Yeah, I did. And after I made that decision and allowed that to happen, I made more money in the first year than I had made the previous 36 years of my life. That was just one little aspect of it.

That's what we meant earlier when we said that everything that you desire is in your vibrational reality—we call that your Vortex. And the Source within you knows where it all is, and also knows the path of least resistance to lead you to it. And it's not getting to the end result that it is really all about, but instead it is the path that is so fun, along the way.

So when you came into this physical body, there was that trajectory that we're talking about, that trajectory of Well-Being. Let's call it the path of least resistance. One of ease. One of fun. One of following your bliss. One of joy. Most of the world doesn't like the idea of following the path of least resistance. To them it just seems like laziness.

So you take a little tributary where you choose some other things. And you give it everything you've got. But the whole time you do it, you can feel that your natural path is calling you. And ultimately the trajectory of *who-you-really-are* always, always wins.

What takes you all so long to relax and give in to your natural Well-Being? It's that you're listening to the others who have all the lists of things that you need to do in order to please them, instead of listening to what the Source within you knows.

Something you said earlier hit a chord: when you said that I am a teacher. You must have said that to me five or six times before. And throughout this entire thing, I said over and over, "*I am a teacher.* I'm not an employee; I am not somebody to be told where to go or how I'm going to do it."

"I am an extension of Source Energy, who has practiced my vibrational frequency into such alignment with my true nature that anything less than that feels off to me. And because I care about the way I feel, I guide myself easily now toward the things that feel good. And therefore, I am always on my path." [Abraham addresses audience] And this book will lead you to yours.

And the things that feel good, sometimes we confuse like it's safer or it's easier. But it doesn't feel so good inside.

Safer feels better than fear or danger, and so it's a step in the right direction. But you don't want to hang around for long reaching for safety, because you can get a vibration going and then other things that are like that show up. In other words, this is a self-course that you are all on. And you have Source Energy guiding you every step of the way. And when you find something that feels good, go that way.

DOOMED TO MAKE CHOICES?

— • ● • —

I had a great teacher in my life, Carl Jung. I was studying early to be a Jungian analyst. He said, "At the same moment that you're a protagonist in your own life and you're making choices, at the very same moment, you're also the spear carrier or the extra in a much larger drama." He said, "All of you are doomed to make choices." And it sounds like such a contrast. If you're doomed, how could you be making choices?

But within our physical bodies, we're doomed. I mean, Esther showed up in a female body of a certain height and certain color hair and certain things. And I showed up in a 6'1" male body and hair is falling out and growing in my ears and all of the crazy things that are happening to it. And I'm just watching it.

But I also have choices to make about this body. I can feed it well. I can exercise it. I can do so many things. So I'm making choices within sort of a doomed state. But what about the other part of us, the spiritual side of us?

Well, we can understand how someone who is trying to explain to someone who is, in this moment, not on the high-flying disc, why they may use words like *doomed*.

Right. He didn't mean it in a, you know—

Meaning that there are unwanted choices. But what we have noticed is that as you sift through the details of your life for a longer and longer time, and more personal preferences are born within you, you become clearer and clearer about *who-you-are* and what you want. And then that is usually when we begin to meet you, because now you are beginning to desire the ability to have more control in your own reality. You just don't know how to go about it.

This is a new conversation that we are having these days with our physical friends because we want you to understand that in your physical form you intended to explore more contrast than we do from our Non-Physical vantage point. And from the contrast comes more detailed desire for improvement in this time-space reality. The evolution of all species is dependent upon that contrasted experience.

But often, as humans explore the contrast, you make comparisons about it such as "These are good manifestations" or "These are bad manifestations," and then you believe that everyone should come to an agreement on things—which really does defy the intentions that all of you held when you came into your physical bodies. That sort of thinking creates a shortage of consciousness within you, and then most just fight over the spoils of physical human life rather than tapping into the Energy that creates worlds, and really loving the life that you have come to live.

When you don't feel good, it is understandable why you would be comparing and measuring experiences in an effort to decide what is the right way to live. But we would like you to just for a little while accept that you are vibration. Accept that you are Source Energy in physical bodies. Accept that you are offering a vibration, and that that vibration is being responded to by *Law of Attraction.*

Accept that the opinion of Source and the opinion of you as you are focused in this moment provide a Guidance System for you that could help you to get back online with *who-you-really-are* and with what you came into this body intending to live.

Now that sounds a little bit like you're a puppet on a string and that Source Energy has already defined what you're supposed to live, but that isn't what we mean at all. Your sifting through the contrast of your physical life has caused you to expand, and your *Inner Being* has become the vibrational equivalent of all of that expansion. So when you care about the way you feel and you come into alignment with what feels good, you also become that expanded version right here and now. And then the first thing you feel is clarity. Clarity about which way to go. Clarity about whether to do this or not. Clarity about whether to have this conversation. Clarity about whether to invest in that, whether to marry them! Clarity. Because Broader Perspective knows *who-you-are,* knows everything about you, and is offering a very strong, very clear opinion.

But you've got to practice tuning in to the vibrational frequency of your Source if you want to have keen awareness of that Guidance. And the alternative is really miserable, because those around you are all wanting different things from you. "Go this way." "Go this way." "Go this way." "Go this way." "Go this way."

Being on Your Path

If you know that you have a dharma, you have a destiny, you have this something, like perhaps you're a great artist. For me, it was a teacher. For me, it was a writer. Things that I have absolute—

For you, it is an uplifter. For you, it is a keeper of the light so that others may find it.

But when I got off that path, when I got away from it, some of the most profound changes in my life occurred, when I was at those lowest places in my life.

Yes, of course, because you don't know what you do want until you know what you don't want. And some of that contrast launches some very big rockets. And it also puts you in touch with your *Emotional Guidance System,* so that you can tell when you're on and when you're off your path.

Is this Source Energy, like, preprogrammed if you will? That you have something that you are supposed to accomplish here in this time? I know *accomplish* isn't the right word . . .

It's not like that. You have come for freedom, growth, and joy.

And when you're away from that, when you're on a path that's taking you away from freedom, from joy, from love—

That sucks.

Yes. But does Divine Guidance come into your life at that time and say, "Okay . . ."

Divine Guidance is in your life all the time, all the time, all the time. Divine Guidance never goes away. It's just that the contrast makes you listen more. Esther has found alignment that she didn't know was possible because of the discomfort she felt when Jerry made his transition. It was miserable at first, but feels worth it now.

Yeah. I was being interviewed by the *New York Times* and Arthur Miller was there. Arthur Miller was a great American playwright, you know; most of you know *Death of a Salesman, The Crucible,* and so on. He was almost 90 years old. And he was asked the question by the interviewer, "Are you working on another play?" And I've never forgotten what he said, because it really resonated with me. He said, "I don't know, but I probably am." Meaning, I think, that there's something else moving these checkers around in this checker game that we're playing.

Well, here's how it works. Life causes you to continue to ask, and as you do, you continue to put those desires and preferences into a vibrational reality that you are not yet cashing in. So, yes, he's going to write another play. It's already there in vibrational reality. And when he stops talking about how tired he is and stops fussing over how incorrectly they handle his material and gets a good night's sleep, he'll wake up with an impression or an inspiration and off he'll go again.

Exactly what I did with this last book. On June the 26th I announced to my kids that I'm not writing any more books. I'm done writing. I've done enough. I don't have to prove myself. I've done 40 books and so on. June 27th I woke up and I was writing. Five months, I wrote morning, noon, and night, until I put my neck out of joint. I mean, I could not stop the writing.

You just have to accept that your Vortex has enough content in it to keep you busy for 20 or 30 lifetimes. And as long as you're having fun, then isn't that the point?

Yeah, it was fun. It was just great joy, as it is to be with you.

IS OVERCOMING
OBSTACLES NECESSARY?

●◦●

I was thinking about this Guidance and about being able to see more clearly now in my life. It took a lot of years and a lot of time, a lot of experiences for me to be able to step back and to see that the right people were showing up at the right time, and that the Guidance was there. And that you have to have kind of a willingness to listen and a determination to not allow other people to dictate to you what your life's purpose is.

I was talking to Esther backstage that just this afternoon I watched the movie called *Jobs*, the story of Steve Jobs. And while he behaved in a pretty crass way to many people, there was an absolute knowing within him that this is the way this industry has to go, or this is the way this company must be run.

And he felt a certain level of frustration, because he knew he was in alignment but was not able to convince the others because they were not in a place where they could hear him.

And sometimes we find ourselves, like in relationships . . . I was in a relationship with my wife for many, many years, and we separated 13 years ago. It was one of the most-trying times in my life, probably as close as I ever was to depression. And yet it isn't always just the things that smell good and the things that look right and the things that make you feel right that cause you to make those right turns and those about-faces and so on. Sometimes it's these enormous obstacles. And you have to almost be fearless in—

Well, we want to tease all of you a little bit by saying to you that if you were more unwilling to put up with negative emotion, your lives would go a whole lot better for you. You have trained yourselves to be willing to endure misalignment. And then you make decisions without the clarity that you're talking about.

And then you seem to have to go down that path a little ways, until after a while, you just get tired of feeling bad. That is true regarding the conversation that we had with you about your father, and it certainly is true about how Esther felt when Jerry made his transition into Non-Physical. And we don't think the stakes should have to be that high. We don't think you should have to let so much bad-feeling momentum mount before you recognize that you could have it another way.

So sometimes it's like to be in a state almost of gratitude for the hardships?

Staying in a state of appreciation would take care of everything because appreciation is the way the Source within you feels all the time, about everything. So it would be constant, continual, chronic alignment.

And it was because of those moments of despair, when I began to be grateful instead of feeling sorry for myself, that I became a much more compassionate person. And my writing took on a whole new flavor. In fact, it was when I wrote *The*

Power of Intention—which probably 50 percent of it was impacted by your teachings, by the Teachings of Abraham; it's all over that book—that I was very deep into not allowing myself to continue down the path of despair.

And when people are in relationships, or in places or in jobs or whatever it is that nothing but despair is showing up, they feel the risk about changing, getting out of it, moving along—

But once you understand the correlation between how you are feeling and the thoughts that you are thinking, which are the reason you feel the way you do, then you can change the way you feel by changing the thoughts you are thinking. And then events change, too. Then you are off and running. It is just a matter of practicing your thoughts on purpose. Think and feel. Think and feel.

It's almost as if different people start showing up in your life, different circumstances. Carl Jung called it synchronicity.

It depends on what vibrational disc you are on. If you're on the ornery disc, ornery people show up. If you're on the high-flying disc, high-flying people show up. If you're on the feel-sorry-for-me disc, feels-sorry-for-me-disc people show up. *Law of Attraction* never gets it wrong.

So God will send you smarter people if you stop thinking in dumb ways.

For example: Because you know what you don't want, you then are able to know what you do want. But the awareness of what you do want is not a very practiced thought yet. You may have only realized it just now. What you do not want, for now, is a much stronger vibration within you. And so it would actually be illogical for you to suddenly begin thinking entirely differently about what you do want, because it is not your pattern of thought.

And so you think more about what you don't want, which causes you to launch another rocket of what you do want, and another and another and another until over time there is quite a gap between what you are actually living and what you are asking for. There is a gap between what is manifesting in your experience and the new vibrational version of yourself.

Sometimes, if your desire is very strong, in a moment when you are not arguing for your limitations or noticing what is missing from your life, you can catch a glimpse of *who-you-really-are*. We like to say that your *Inner Being* is always there with the expanded version of you keeping the light on for you to help you find it.

So let's say you have a lot of friends, and they're all over the place in terms of the way they feel, and you are, too. Sometimes you hang out in a good-feeling place together, but not usually. But then you begin to understand your own *Guidance System*. And you care about the way that you feel. You begin waking up and deliberately focusing upon good-feeling thoughts long enough that other good-feeling thoughts are joining them. And in time, you are able to stay there consistently.

So then, even though your friends may be up and down and all around, you are consistently feeling better. So when they do rendezvous with you, they will be in a more receptive mode to what you are helping them to understand.

That is what your *Inner Being* has been doing all along—staying in that higher vibration. It is because your *Inner Being* is already in the place of knowing that you have those aha moments when you get it. You get it when you align with your *Inner Being*. It is through your own life experience that your awareness comes, because words, in and of themselves, do not teach.

Inundated with
Bad News

• ● •

It seems like we get almost inundated with bad news, you know, like what we watch on the television . . .

If you're on the bad-news disc, you are.

Well, I find in the last few years, especially the closer I get to what I think of as Divine love, living from a place of oneness, that I'm not nearly as interested in hearing the news, or in hearing other people's sad stories.

A horrible thing just happened in the Philippines where they estimate that maybe 10,000 people are dead. But to continuously watch the violence and the horrors of the world . . .

Most people do not realize that watching the violence and horrors of the world causes you to practice the vibration of it. And once you have practiced the vibration of it, you are going to rendezvous with more of it. And it doesn't mean that you are going to immediately have that horrible experience, but it does mean that more experiences like that are going to come into your consciousness, and that your sense of Well-Being will be muted.

People protest to us, saying that they cannot just put their head in the sand and be oblivious to what is going on in the world. And we say we would be a selective sifter. We would do our best to see our world through the eyes of Source—because Source is looking at the expansion. Source is looking at what is wanted.

When you define that you want something, Source looks there. And when you look in opposition to what you have defined for Source, you separate yourself from Source.

The vibrational frequency of a question and the vibrational frequency of the answer are very different frequencies. Also the vibrational frequencies of a problem and a solution are very different. So since Source is always on the solution frequency, when you are not, you are not going to feel good, and also you cannot receive inspiration from Source. You will, however, from that contrasting place of not feeling good, launch more rockets of desire, and good does come from that. But it doesn't have to be so hard for so many of you.

CARING ABOUT
HOW YOU FEEL?

• ● •

Do you have to constantly be aware of your thoughts? I mean they just come and—

No, but you do have to care about how you feel, because if you care about how you feel, when you start down the track that is not in keeping with the Source within you, you'll feel the emptiness. Emptiness is a good description, because that's exactly what it is. You have diverged from what Source thinks about this.

That's amazing, because years ago when I first got a cell phone, I had to put an outgoing message on it, and I was very heavy into your work at that time. And so it said, "This is Wayne Dyer that you've reached. And I want to feel good. So if your message is designed to do anything other than that, you've reached the wrong number. Perhaps then you want to call Dr. Phil or someone, you know, who wants to hear bad news." And that's still my message on my answering machine, because I want to feel good.

That's the message that Source has, too.

Right. So when we're having thoughts that don't make us feel good—we're in a relationship with someone that doesn't feel good; we're in a job that doesn't feel good—is Source Energy going to offer us some experiences that are going to match up to what we are thinking that is feeling bad, feeling horrible?

It isn't Source that's giving it to you. There are no lessons being applied.

Well, I mean certain people show up in your life experiences, synchronistic kinds of things.

Things are always working out for you—always.

So it's like your gauge is to look at your feelings. What does this feel like in my body? And if it doesn't feel good, instantly go back to whatever thought it is that I'm having that is allowing this to take place? I mean, can we all just always feel good all the time?

The way we like to explain it is that when you offer a thought about anything, Source, who is always walking with you, thinking with you, living with you, is having a thought about the same thing.

That's really important to hear.

And when you feel good, your thought is in sync with the way Source thinks about it. And when you feel bad, you're off the track of what Source knows about it. And you also have to understand that you are the one who launched the desire to begin with. You are the one who told Source *who-you-are* and what you want. In other words, you are the creator of your own reality. Source is the one who holds the vibrational frequency of what you're asking for.

It's not possible for you to desire something that would be detrimental to anyone, and feel good at the same time, because if you set forth an intention like that, you would deviate from the vibration of Source and you would feel the emptiness of it, you see.

So it really is all about caring about the way you feel, about thinking more deliberately and about keeping an ear to the ground about how you feel.

And if you don't feel good?

Don't worry; it will get bigger.

What will get bigger?

The thought will get bigger, and the awareness that you have diverged from *who-you-really-are* will get bigger. Your uncomfortable emotion will get stronger.

And ultimately, you'll just walk away from that? You'll leave that situation? I'm thinking about again the movie I saw this afternoon about Steve Jobs where he didn't feel good about the way things were going in the working of his company. He just had an absolute knowing, which I've had my whole life, an absolute knowing about how to do what I do. And I listen nicely—because I'm

nicer than Steve Jobs was—to people who tell me how I should be doing things. But inside, there's this absolute knowing that I can't veer away from.

True masters have figured out how to access this Energy that creates worlds. They know what leverage feels like. And they get hooked on it. And so when you're accustomed to things moving in big ways, because you've accessed this Energy, because you've figured out how to stop shooting yourself in the foot and you've practiced it, and you've allowed the momentum to get going, then when you deviate from it, you take it pretty hard and you know it.

He reached the place, and many of you do, where you just get tired of trying to convince people who are on different vibrational discs what you mean. In other words, he reached the place where he realized, and accurately, that if he were to try to convince them of the course that he believed was right, that he would lose his own alignment. And he wasn't willing to do that. And so he stepped away, created a whole other company, found vibrational alignment. And eventually, things came back around to him.

The way we like to explain it is most physical beings live in a world where they're trying to please each other. They have given their *Guidance System* away long ago. Because when your mother or someone holds you as her object of attention and approves of what you do, it feels good to you. So you keep trying to do things that will make her feel approval, which feels good to you, without realizing that every step along that way, you are giving up your potential awareness of your own Guidance that is coming forth from within.

So a lot of people come to believe in action and words and group consensus. And, of course, those things do create to a certain degree. But compared to those who tap into this Energy Stream, that is very mediocre creating. So there are a lot of people who learn to be *nice* because it's expected of them. And we're not saying that you can't be *nice* in all situations, but we are saying that it is normal to feel bad when you are focused in opposition to *who-you-really-are* and what you really want. And it is not possible to convince yourself that you feel good when you don't.

And that's what you witnessed in that documentary. He wasn't willing to pretend that he was in that leverage that he was so accustomed to when he was not. And so he just stepped back and said, "Fine, you all do it the way you want to do it. Because you are marching to the beat of a different drummer than I am." And eventually they came back begging him to assist them because they missed the energy and clarity and power that his focus brought to the whole experience.

After I declared that I wasn't writing another book and that I was done with that and I was tired and I didn't have to do that anymore, then I wrote for five straight months every single day. And now I'm already writing another book and that one isn't even published yet.

There is no end to your books. Just give in to it. Just give in to it.

I explained in one of the chapters of *I Can See Clearly Now* how when I was a boy, while everyone else was watching Milton Berle, Mr. Tuesday Night, Mr. Comedy, I was watching a show by a Catholic bishop, Bishop Sheen. It was called *Life Is Worth Living.* I was 12 years old, 13 years old, and I was actually taking notes on this show, because I just loved it. I had a stepfather for a few years and he was Catholic and he would turn this thing on, so there was no Milton Berle where I lived. But I couldn't wait for Tuesday night. I am fascinated that at that young age I was taking notes from a show called *Life Is Worth Living.*

Because?

Well, I've written 40 books that could have had that subtitle.

But you were 13 years old and doing that because . . . ?

Because it seems to me now, as I step back, I didn't know it at the time—

But the point we are making is that, at that time, you were doing it because it felt good to you.

This is what I was here for.

It was clarity. He was a man tuned in, tapped in, turned on, offering a vibration. You listened to him long enough to feel some resonance with it. It called you back. A very important piece in the unfolding of that which is you. He was tuning you to the frequency of your Source.

Was this celestial guidance?

It always is. It always is. None of you are here alone. All of you are powerful creators. All of you are meaningful and important. All of you have come with great reason and purpose. And if you don't feel fabulous, you have deviated from the path of *who-you-really-are*. It's time to wake up in the morning and reach for the high-flying disc and train yourself back onto it in order to be *who-you-are*.

So for everybody, everybody watching, everybody here, it's like when there's something inside of you that's calling . . . It's like, I just think of it as a calling.

But for you to be able to hear the calling, you have to have practiced yourself into the frequency. And then that calling that you are speaking about feels like inspiration. In other words, that's when you start realizing it, you see. By the time you feel the calling, you've been in the frequency long enough that you're starting to translate it into something that's meaningful for you. And that's a self-taught course.

Yeah. It's interesting, because now this thing that I'm writing, I mean, I took the *Tao Te Ching*, a famous book written 2,500 years ago, and wrote my interpretations of it in a book when I turned 65 eight years ago. And now I have a place on

Maui. And I had four things that I had to do. I had to stop at the Safeway to get some gift cards because I was going to see my kids. I had to stop at the bank to get some cash—

Because you were going to see your kids.

Because I was going to see my kids. You have to take lots of cash for that. I had to stop at the vitamin store because I wanted to pick up some supplements because I was going on this trip— this is a part of that trip. And I wanted to stop at another store that sells something called Poke, which is this wonderful Hawaiian food that I love. And then I was going to go home. That was my plan. But instead, my car actually drove me. I wasn't driving. I don't even know how to say this. I was just—

You were inspired to behavior that wasn't coming from your conscious mind, because you were in vibrational accord with Broader Perspective, who knows *who-you-really-are* and where you really meant to go.

Right. So it took me to Barnes & Noble, and I'm halfway out of the car and all of a sudden I

think, *What am I doing here at Barnes & Noble? I've got to get back. I've got a flight to catch.* But instead of moving toward my flight, I've got this classic text in my hand. It's called the Bhagavad Gita that was written, again, 2,500 or so years ago.

Now fast-forward for a little bit and imagine being in the clarity that you're in now, walking through Barnes & Noble and knowing that there's something really important there for you, feeling that clarity about it. In other words, you stumbled into it and you did know it when you saw it, but wouldn't you like that clarity every step of the way?

I would. I do have that clarity. But not every step. But a lot of them and lot more than I used to. So there I am looking through various things on the Bhagavad Gita because it is clearly a calling. I just think that this ancient text has been misinterpreted in so many ways.

Like all ancient texts. You could give the ancient texts up since you have access to Source Energy now. Right now, all of you.

INTERPRETING THE BHAGAVAD GITA

I want to ask you something from there, okay? The Bhagavad Gita is a simple story of Arjuna, a man who's getting ready to go to battle—

Low-flying disc.

Right. And his charioteer is Krishna, who turns out to be Source Energy, God, all right, whatever.

[Playfully] No, not while on a low-flying disc.

Well, in the Gita, all right. So, he's being given this advice and so much of it is in alignment with what you say, Abraham. But there's a point in there that has so troubled me. I've read the entire Bhagavad Gita three times now in the last couple of months and I don't even know why. I just keep reading it, and going through it, and taking notes on it, and writing.

Maybe it's because the original authors would like to help you clear it up and write it the way it was meant to be heard.

Maybe. I don't know. But there is a point where he's ready to go to battle and he has said that this is his duty. And Krishna, Source Energy, supposedly God, says to him, Go and do your duty. If it means killing people, then that's your duty because you don't get to kill anybody. I take all life; I'm responsible for all life. And he goes off into battle, you know, to do his duty.

So my question to you, Abraham, is: Do we have duties that involve doing things that are inconsistent with Divine love?

Never. But when you're on the low-flying disc, it is from that vibrational stance that you are doing your interpreting. Here's how it works. So let's say that you get on the disc of revenge or worry or insecurity, and you stay there for a while. You read about it, you talk with other people about it, and so you get a lot of momentum going. The significant factor is you get a lot of momentum going.

So you have created a vibrational frequency which is your point of attraction: Perhaps the frequency of despair, or the frequency of orneriness, or the frequency of hope, or the frequency of love. As you spend a little bit of time on a disc, *Law of Attraction* produces more momentum. So when you get on the disc of revenge and you talk with others about it and you fan the flames of your revenge talking about how you've been wronged, as others join you the momentum gets even stronger. Eventually enough momentum happens that you receive what feels to you like an inspiration to take action. That is momentum. It's the force of something that is moving in the direction that it has been moving.

But we promise you, that type of momentum which is born out of what you do not want and which is accompanied by negative emotion is not inspiration coming from Source Energy. Source never joins you on the revenge disc, ever. But we can see how it feels like it, because the revenge sure felt better than being taken advantage of, and it sure felt better to overtake them than to be overtaken by them. But there is another way, you see.

And so there are a lot of people who are living their lives doing things that they would say "are just my job." But in fact, their jobs involve a lot of violence, a lot of hatred, a lot of killing, a lot of things that are inconsistent with higher awareness, higher Consciousness. And justifying it on the basis of what Krishna is saying to Arjuna, which is "This is your duty. You don't get to take life. I take all life. And all life is given by me, speaking as God or Source."

We are not taking issue with anything that anyone decides that they want to do. We're not saying that one behavior is wrong while another behavior is right. But we are saying, unless you are in sync with the Source within you, the behavior that you're offering is not inspired—it is motivated. It is not coming from Source; it is coming from the spinoff of Man's conscious mind.

In other words, Source would never guide you to negative behavior toward any other. And if you feel that you're being guided toward negative behavior toward others, you've just got momentum going on a lower-flying disc.

Well, one soldier a day commits suicide.

Because he is off the trajectory of who he really knows himself to be. He can't bear that behavior.

Here's what we would do. So here you stand. You are listening in on this, all of you. And we're having a very in-depth, truly Leading Edge conversation about it. And so you think about soldiers who are doing their duty. And you want to feel patriotic and you want to appreciate them for their sacrifices and you appreciate the things that they're doing on behalf of your nation. Well, those feelings feel good to you. Those are good-feeling thoughts. So that's the aspect of that which you want to focus upon. But let's say that you are aware that truly awful things are happening to people in villages somewhere. And when you focus upon those things, it takes you to your knees, because it is such a departure from *who-you-really-are.*

So what do you do? Do you hide your head in the sand? Do you condemn those who are doing it? Or do you let this contrasting experience help you define what you want, and do you then line up with that?

Do you then begin telling the story of a world that is more compassionate? Do you speak of the people of a world who are understanding more clearly who they are, of a world where all children are eating, where children are waking up and feeling secure in their own beds, where parents are waking up and understanding that the world is big enough for everyone.

In other words, you can beat the drum of dysfunction and it is an easy thing to do in this world with all of this media. But it never feels good to you when you do it. And you do have the ability to make choices, and when you do, you will discover your true power, because one who is connected to the Stream is more powerful than millions who are not, you see.

Oh, that's so true.

So, if you hold your vision of what you want relative to the war, or whatever the uncomfortable situation is, and so you are able to align yourself with Source, you will feel inspiration. You do not have to travel to that part of the world, you do not have to participate in the action of the war, you don't have to send your dollars. When you align with Source Energy while focusing upon the subject of your desire, you are trading in a vibrational currency.

When you sync up with Source, holding those things as your object of attention, people who are there who are also tired of war, who also understand that war is not the answer, may have an opportunity of picking up on that path of least resistance that you have carved out, and an idea may be born within them.

I see a lot of that. I mean, I get a lot of mail from people who are—

Many want to change the world, but the world doesn't need to be changed. If you believe the world needs to be changed, in your struggle and effort you prevent your alignment with Source, who allows you the means to change it. You must come into alignment and then focus your attention on the improvements you desire. Get on the high-flying disc and then focus.

SPENDING CURRENCY OF THOUGHT

---•◉•---

In my talks I often give this example: If I gave you a currency of a million dollars, and I said go out and spend this on everything that you want, go to the mall and buy anything that you want. So you begin walking through stores and every store you go into, you buy something that you don't like. You buy ten of these and fifty of these. And you get home and you ask, "Why is my house filled with so much stuff that I don't want?" Then I say the answer is "Because you're crazy."

Because you tried to fill the void with action. You're looking for love in all the wrong places. You tried to fill the void with action and things rather than through alignment. And that doesn't mean that in alignment you won't be inspired to want some things. But if the inspiration comes from alignment, they will be meaningful things.

Right. But isn't so much of our inner attention not only on what we don't want, but on what other people want for us, or it's on how things used to be, or it's even on *what-is.* **I mean if you don't like** *what-is,* **and your thoughts are on** *what-is,* **it seems to me that you're going to just create more and more of** *what-is.*

It comes from the belief that you should face reality. Most people offer most of their vibration in response to what they are observing. So they observe it; they offer a vibration; they get more of it. And so, of course, then they believe it. But when you realize that you have the option of focusing on things that you really want, and that those things will come to you, too, then you are a Deliberate Creator rather than a creator by default.

It is a wonderful thing when you realize how quickly *Law of Attraction* responds to your vibration.

But it is an even more wonderful thing when you realize that *Law of Attraction* is responding to your vibration, and that you can feel the alignment/resonance or misalignment/discord of *Law of Attraction* responding to the Source within you.

As you have been expanding and evolving, the Source within you is beating the drum of *who-you-are*. And there is a powerful trajectory of wonderful things flowing to you. And when you get off the track from that, you really feel it in the form of negative emotion. And when you relax and let yourself get back on the track, then you feel your clarity. Then you feel your abundance. Then you feel your worthiness. Then you feel your fun and vitality and eagerness and passion. Then life is good for you, just the way you intended.

ARE THERE ASCENDED MASTERS?

•●•

Are there ascended masters out there? I mean, we hear so much about people like St. Germaine and Jesus . . .

Well, this alignment is not like a college degree where once you achieve it, it is yours forevermore. It either is or it isn't in the moment. But there certainly are those who catch the spirit of that alignment and work to maintain it. And that is what you are talking about.

Can we access these people?

They're available to you at all times. Just get focused on what they are interested in, and see how readily available they are to you.

And what are they interested in?

Everything that you are interested in. They're eager. You see, this physical time-space reality is the Leading Edge of thought. Humans often think that this is just a trial ground and that heaven is where it's at. But this is the Leading Edge of thought. This is where thought manifests. This is where it is at.

Earth is crammed with heaven.

Earth is heaven. Or hell. Your choice.

Is There a Hell?

• ● •

And speaking of hell, does such a thing exist?

Only in the minds of disconnected humans. The animals don't know of it. Only humans who pinch themselves off from clarity. Wouldn't you call confusion a sort of hell? Wouldn't you call lethargy a sort of hell?

People who have behaved in horrific ways, is there punishment when they leave this earthly plane?

Humans are often disappointed when we tell them that is not the case. Your punishment is self-inflicted as you deprive yourself of the Energy of Source, which is available to you at all times. When you disallow that, it is very unpleasant. But when you reemerge back into Non-Physical, you will leave behind all doubt and fear, all grudges, all hatred, all misunderstanding. And you will become a vibrational equivalent to all that this life and before has caused you to become.

ABOUT PAST REGRETS

---●●●---

As I was writing my book *I Can See Clearly Now*, I thought of the low points in my life and things I had done, my behavior, my consciousness . . .

Yes, but how would you know you are seeing clearly if you did not have the experience of not seeing clearly? How would you appreciate clarity or even recognize it?

That's a very good point.

You would not have the clarity that you have found if you hadn't lived in some of that. And how can you live other than what you are living? Source has always been right there, calling you forward.

From where you now stand, you often look back and condemn former experiences you have lived, saying you shouldn't have been on that path or you shouldn't have lived that experience. But really, Source called you every step along the way—because it was the path of least resistance and, therefore, was the only path that was available to you at the time.

It's a good thing to give yourselves a break. Source is not judging you. You do it to yourself. And then you pinch yourself off from Source.

When I think of the ways that I have behaved at earlier times in my life, I think, I've just been lucky, because had I been found out . . .

But things are always working out for you. And your behavior didn't deserve punishment. It didn't deserve finding out. You were just off your path a little bit. Source is always looking the other way when you stumble. Never looking at what you think is wrong. That's you who do that to yourselves and to each other.

When a little child is just learning to walk and falls down, you don't disapprovingly say, "Get up, you little dummy!" You understand that falling down is the way he learns to find his balance. And Source feels the same way about all of you.

So I can feel good about some of those experiences?

You'd better if you want to be on your high-flying disc.

Right.

You cannot look back with any condemnation of self without disconnecting yourself from Source, who feels good about everything you've lived.

Everything?

Everything.

I've often said that true nobility is not about being better than anyone else; it's about being better than you used to be. And in every regard, I think I am better than I used to be.

Nobility's overrated. It is a human term. God never uses the term *nobility*, ever. What does *noble* mean, anyway?

Well, you know, it's like we're talking now: perfection.

Yes, but there isn't any of that because you never get it done. Perfection smacks of endedness, and there isn't any of that. So nobility is another of those things that humans use to compare themselves with each other while they are on lower-flying discs.

CAN YOU SHARE A SOUL?

• ● •

**This thing inside of us that we call a soul—
can you share a soul with another person?**

Well, it is Consciousness, and it is a Stream.
Esther can feel as she reaches for Abraham that we
are a Collective Consciousness. She can feel a difference in emphasis sometimes. She can feel a stronger
emphasis right now in this conversation because of
what you are calling forth. Here's a good way of explaining it. When Jerry made his transition, Esther
had been hearing from Abraham for a long time.
She was very comfortable with the idea of Abraham
and with the vibrational relationship she had with

Abraham. She trusts us. She knows the feeling of us. She can feel the fullness of us.

And when Jerry made his transition, she didn't want him to just go be part of the Abraham soup. Of course, he is part of the Abraham soup, but she wants to carve him out in a special way. She has already known Abraham. Now she wants Jerry to obviously be Jerry. She wants him to be interested in the track titles for this conversation that we're having. She wants him to be interested in this piece of furniture that she's buying, because he always said, "Let's not junk it up." And she worries that she might be junking it up a little bit as she buys one more thing and drags it home.

And so she's interested in what he thinks about all of that. And because of who she knew him to be, and who she now knows him to be, she can feel the specifics of that which is Jerry from the Non-Physical that is flowing through her.

But the most important thing is that Esther had to forget who Jerry was in order to find who he now is. He is no longer pushing against things that he did not like. Many things that he felt very strongly about while in his physical body are no longer of concern to him.

And how do you know it?

By allowing him to train her into his new perspective. It was necessary to let go of some of the active vibrations that she remembered about him when he was physical in order to find him now in the Non-Physical. And because she wanted so much to find him, she was able to do that. And in doing so, she's finding her own *Inner Being* in a stronger way.

That was a surprise to Esther. She has been living happily ever after for a long time, following what she considered to be a wise man who was always loving and kind and always good to everyone. She let him take the lead and she followed in pure bliss. But now she is discovering that he wants her to lead, and that he revels in the alignment that she finds.

Is this done through a feeling?

Yes. When Jerry was in his physical body and Jerry and Esther were having a conversation, she would say, "I really want to know what you think about this." And he would say, "I don't think you really want to know what I think. I think you want me to agree with what you think about it." And that was sorta kinda true.

Where now she's not interested in him agreeing with her. She really wants to know what he thinks.

She wants to train her vibration into that Pure, Positive Energy, you see.

Does he give her signals when he's around? Does the furniture move? Do things fall off the bookcase?

We were talking earlier with you about how even though you had a big wad of resistance relative to your father, the power of your desire eventually led to that wonderful moment of forgiveness and your coming back into complete alignment. And so this experience of Jerry and Esther will tell you a lot.

Not long after Jerry had made his transition, Esther was really having a hard day. She was visiting with her sister Jeanne, saying out loud to her, "Where is Jerry? He said that he would show up. Where is he? I want to know where he is. I can't find him. Where is he?"

And at that moment, the *Sara* book—Esther wrote a series of *Sara* books which present the Teachings of Abraham through a fictional story about a girl named Sara—on the shelf right where Jerry had placed it, slapped right down on the shelf. Esther knew that Jerry was making his presence known to her in the moment of her extremely powerful desire. That was about two years ago, but now Esther knows that Jerry will not play that silly game with her. In other words, now she knows that she must be in alignment with who she is in order to interact with him.

Their house is U-shaped and there is a light in the bedroom that Esther can see from the bedroom, from the living room, from her office looking across the pool. It is a light that shines down on a quartz rock wall, and Esther can see it from just about every room she spends time in.

Often, when she is really feeling good, that light blinks in appreciation of her joy. But if she ever feels sad or lonely and sits looking at the light, saying, "Blink the light," the light does not blink. He will not come down to a lower disc to play with her. If she's going to play with him, she's got to get up there where she belongs and where he is.

When I make my transition, will I be able to make contact with the people I love?

Yes, everyone that you care about.

Do you set an intention before? Because I've been doing that.

Yes, but it is not only because of intentions that you set before you make your transition. From your Non-Physical vantage point, you have keen interest in what is happening on Earth.

We in the Non-Physical are multidimensional. We are Consciousness, and whenever you—in your physical form—focus, we are always there with you, no exceptions. But it is necessary that you tune yourself to the recognition of us.

Think about your teachings and the books that you have written. When you are no longer here in your physical body and have reemerged back into Non-Physical, as people are reading your books, you will be aware of that. You will tap into that.

This is a big concept for humans to get their thoughts around. You sometimes feel overwhelmed with the idea of that. For a little while after Jerry made his transition into Non-Physical, Esther felt jealous because while he was in his physical body, she had his undivided attention. But now he is visiting with many.

The frequency is always there and can be received by you, but for you to *realize* it, you've got to be up to speed with it. And when you are, then that clarity that you were talking about, that realization, happens to you.

TRUSTING IN YOURSELF?

I've often said, "When you trust in yourself, you are trusting in the wisdom that created you."

And how do you do that? You've got to feel your way to it, don't you? Because if you learned it from your mother, she wasn't all that trustworthy. She sometimes was in a really bad mood when she told you what to do.

And so you have to train yourself into trusting. It is about practicing the good-feeling thoughts until you are able to continually align with your Broader Self, or as you are saying, with the wisdom that created you.

If you practice the vibrations of this high-flying disc so that you are doing it on purpose, when you begin slipping from it, you will recognize that you are slipping and then you can do something about it. In time, with practice, you can get control of your own vibration. And when you get control of your own vibration, the first thing that happens is your sense of self-worth comes into place—because the entire Universe is assisting you. You feel clarity, and everything works out. It's like a concierge leading you everywhere that you want to go. There are no missteps. Things no longer feel difficult. In fact, things that at one time felt difficult often feel humorous to you.

Esther knew that she was on the high-flying disc in a more consistent way when one day something had fallen behind a very heavy chest and she couldn't get it out easily. She was laughing as she was trying to engineer how to get it out. Sixty days earlier, she would have been swearing about it. But now Esther is just enjoying figuring out how to fish it out rather than complaining that she has more important things to do than fishing objects out from behind furniture.

Isn't life really about these moments and these moments and these moments? People are waiting for their dream vacation or their dream relationship or their dream car or their dream job. And we say, Later is never going to come, because it is always now, now, now, now, now. *Now* alignment or not. *Now* alignment or not. *Now* alignment or not.

And when you show yourself that you can have *now* alignment, *now* alignment, *now* alignment, now you're living the way you intended to live.

Do you have to almost catch yourself when you're having a thought that's misaligned and correct it? I mean, it seems to me it's stuck in here in our subconscious mind in some way.

It sort of is.

So you get ahold of this thought and you real-ize, *I just had a judgmental thought, so I'm not going to do that again.* But for me, I have to go back and correct the thought. And then I have to correct the behavior.

Yes, but you slow yourself down unnecessarily, because that is going about it the hard way. While you slumber, your momentum stops. Then when you awaken, you are in a state of nonresistance and so it is easier to find the high-flying disc. And then the momentum will increase from that place of

127

nonresistance. It is a much easier way of going about it.

We are not saying that there may not be behavior that you may want to change. Of course there is. Often when you are offering effort about something, you are activating an opposing vibration to your desire. And while you don't mean to be doing it, you are actually practicing the vibration of resistance, rather than the vibration of allowing.

Changing Thoughts and Making Amends

• ◉ •

This conversation may be causing me to change my mind, but I have often thought that making amends, for example, is a way of reprogramming your subconscious mind.

Source never forgives anyone because Source never condemns anybody to begin with.

Doesn't blame in the first place, yeah.

So when you feel the way Source feels about someone, you're in sync with Source. You may call it forgiveness; we call it alignment. And you get hooked on that feeling because it sure feels better to love them than to hate them.

Oh, yeah.

Esther has said to us on more than one occasion, "Well, Abraham, maybe I need to tell you more about that person. It seems to me you're being a little unrealistic in your unconditional love for them."

But, you see, unconditional love is loving because that's what you do. That's *who-you-are*. In conditional love you say, "If you change your behavior, then I will love you." But that is such a trap for you and for them, because now you are trying to figure out which behavior is the appropriate behavior. And no one feels good. You are mad at each other in your disagreements about what is right and what is wrong. And meanwhile, Source is loving all of you and feeling very good.

HIS BLISSFUL HEALING EXPERIENCE

I wanted to ask you: About three years ago, I was diagnosed with leukemia, which, of course, led to a series of experiences. But there is a gentleman on the planet living in Brazil, in Abadiânia, who goes by the name *John of God* in English. Now, who am I to ask you whether entities can enter into somebody else's body? I had this most amazing experience with *John of God*.

Because, like with Jesus, his vibration of Well-Being is dominant. And because your expectation didn't prevent it, you allowed the experience.

I haven't been back to check blood levels or anything like that, because I just go by how I feel, and I feel fine. So many things changed in that. But the major change after having this healing experience with this man who has treated some 40 million people over the last 40 years or so, was that after the experience, things just looked different to me.

Two of my children were with me on Maui and when I walked out of the room and I looked at them, they just looked totally different to me than ever before. They just looked like pure—

You were looking at them through the eyes of Source.

Pure love, yeah. And, I mean, I was weeping. I mean, I put my arms around my daughter and told her how beautiful she is. I was holding my son. I looked at the ocean; it looked like a sea of love, you know. I looked at the palm trees—

You were influenced into alignment.

Yeah, it was so powerful. My 71st birthday was a couple of weeks later and I woke up that morning—I was in San Francisco making a film about my father, called *My Greatest Teacher,* about for-giveness and so on—and all I wanted to do that day was give. I've never had a birthday like this, and I've never forgotten it.

I went downstairs and I had a couple of thou-sand dollars with me and I got $50 bills, a couple of thousand dollars' worth of them, and I went out to Union Square, and from seven o'clock in the morning until about five o'clock in the after-noon, I just embraced homeless people. Little old ladies who were looking for plastic water bottles; people didn't smell very good; people who were . . .

I was just in this state of bliss. It was such a pure love. All I wanted to do was give. I just want-ed to give. I just wanted to serve. And that im-pacted me so much that it's why I wear LOVE on my shirt. It's why I'm writing about Divine love. It's why I'm here speaking to you, who teaches us about something called Divine love. And what a thrill it is for me to just be here in your presence.

When you're told that you have something like leukemia, there is fear associated with it. Not fear of dying so much. But there is so much fear associated with the word *cancer.* Cancer of the blood. And there is so much of it in our society.

I have a dear friend, Anita Moorjani, who has written a book called *Dying to Be Me,* about her near-death experience. She talked about her cancer and how serious it was, and how she was able to come back from it. She said, "It's just all fear. It's just all fear."

It felt like the entities that came to me through *John of God*, came in and took the fear, whatever fear was related to that, and replaced it with love.

We would say it a little differently: The removal part, no. The emphasis on the love part, yes. So that the vibration of Well-Being was dominant.

This is an interesting subject, because everyone who is here in a physical body understands that they are going to make a transition. And yet dying is seen by most humans as an inappropriate thing to do. So if the path of least resistance looks like it's taking you out of your physical body, then you have some personal determination to make about how you feel about being here, in this body.

In other words, when you know clearly what you do not want, it helps you to know clearly what you do want. And when there is a large gap between where you believe you are and where you want to be, it is very uncomfortable. That is what the fear is all about. But when you close that gap, it's a really wonderful feeling of relief.

So we want to put healing in the category of what we are always talking about: *alignment.* But we also want to say that there is a great amount of true alignment that happens in what you call the death experience.

And so what it comes down to is you in your physical body now making a statement of what you intend, because you get to decide. As long as you're having fun, having meaningful experiences, and are enjoying the way life is juxtapositioning you with other things, then there is no reason that you cannot continue to sift through the contrast of this life experience and to give birth to new intentions. And Source will support you in all of that, no matter what.

It really is your choice. But most people, when they think of some illnesses, believe that they are without choice. And that is why you feel fear. You feel fear because you are thinking in opposition to the way Source is viewing your situation. Fear is just the way you feel when you have a different opinion from Source.

So what did *John of God* do for you? You, like everyone else, have access to that Energy Stream. You do not need an intermediary to flow stronger Energy at you. But his attention upon you caused you to focus stronger expectation. In other words, he soothed your vibration of misalignment, and therefore helped you to allow the vibration of alignment.

Say that again. That was so beautiful.

Because of your attention upon him, you found a way of allowing the Energy that was there for you all along to be received by you. He did not receive the Energy and assert it at you. You don't need someone to assert healing Energy. You all have access to that energy. But he helped you to expect it. By virtue of what you have heard about him, and what you know of him, your expectation shifted so that the fear was not there. And in the absence of the fear caused by your focusing upon him, the healing took place.

The healing was such a feeling of love.

Alignment, clarity. The word *clarity* is the best word to describe alignment—clarity, knowing, un-questioning. Yes?

Yes, and *I Can See Clearly Now.* It's one of the signature moments in my life.

Yes, because it felt to you as if the stakes were higher. But the stakes are never really high. In other words, you can be or do or have anything that you want. Source always has your back. It's just that sometimes when the stakes feel higher, you find alignment more deliberately.

It created in me a sense of just wanting to serve. To get my ego out of this.

You cannot **not** serve. When you're tuned in, tapped in, turned on, you are like a satellite dish, so to speak, bringing the signal in closer so that others may have an opportunity to notice it. If you are steadily aligned with that signal of Well-Being, then others have greater opportunities to rendezvous with your beaming of it. In other words, it's what we were talking about earlier. People are zigging and zagging in and out of alignment, and if you are tuned in and not tuned in, and not tuned in, and not tuned in, they don't have as much opportunity to benefit when they rendezvous with you. But when you're consistently there, then they have more opportunity to rendezvous with your positive Connection to Source.

And the most interesting thing about that is, you cannot serve others unless you have first served yourself with your alignment. Because if you're not tuned in to that Energy, you don't have anything to give anyone.

It seems, Abraham, that there's so much cancer, so much dis-ease in our culture, particularly in America, and there's so much fear. And I don't mean fear in the sense of being afraid of dying—

Let's just call it momentum for a while.

Okay.

Just think of it as momentum, and then just watch what's going on around you. Notice the perpetuation of momentum, but also acknowledge that in that knowing of what you do not want, there's also a perpetuation of the solution.

So even though your society is for the most part more in sync with the problem than they are the solution, the solution is in the process of becoming. And more like you are finding alignment with that.

So, if we can get this fear out of it . . . do you think the cancer rates will go down?

For sure, and you found a really good way of saying. You said, "If we can get the fear out of it," and then you stopped yourself.

Right.

The fear is the result of the misalignment. It is to help you to redirect your thoughts toward what you want, and not so much toward what you don't want. But that is going to require a lot of people to be willing to reach for better-feeling frequencies.

And for many of you, until the stakes are really high, most of you are willing to put up with being on the ornery disc. You see, the reason that so much of what you are living is such a departure from what you really want isn't because you are terrible people. It isn't because you've done terrible things. It's because you're chronically holding yourself away from the vibration of alignment that is natural to you. And so just a little bit of attention to the way you feel, and a determination to feel better more of the time, will get you back into alignment with Well-Being.

GENETICALLY MODIFIED FOOD AND MORE

———— • ● • ————

Okay, so there's a big, big, big issue out there for me that creates a lot of—

[Playfully] So, do you want to activate it and add momentum to it and practice the vibration of it?

So it seems . . .

Do you? Do you? Do you? Do you? Do you? Do you? Do you?

[Playfully] Be nice, Steve Jobs. So, it seems to me that the cycle of life is one in which—whether it's in the animal kingdom, whether it's in the vegetable kingdom, whether it's in the human kingdom, or even in the mineral kingdom—the way it works is that this generation's seed provides life to the next generation's seed, to the next generation and the next. And it's like the seed from this plant gives life to the next plant and so on . . .

[Playfully, not wanting to go where Wayne is going with this] We love you so much, yeah, yeah, yeah, yeah, yeah.

Okay. And in humans as well. But what has happened, and there have just been alarmingly drastic shifts in the last generation or two, the number of children born into autism, for example, has gone from 1 in 10,000 to 1 in a 100 in 30 years.

Because, like you, they are coming forth to demand their freedom to be. So they're saying, "I'm going to be so different; you are not going to pound this round peg into a square hole."

Okay. The amount of obesity has increased in our culture dramatically. I do not believe it is because we've become a nation of gluttons. I believe it is that we're starting to genetically modify our food.

Yes. Well, you are looking for love in all the wrong places. You're looking for food that tastes good rather than food that feels good. You're not letting it guide you from your perspective of alignment; you're just looking for a way to fill the void. Don't you notice that when you are at your orneriest or your most dysfunctional that you are often looking for something to eat?

But what has happened is that we've genetically modified this food so that the seed for the next generation doesn't come from the wheat, or it doesn't come from the corn—it comes from Monsanto; it comes from these big companies that have patents on our food. We can't even put it in the ground without getting permission from big companies.

We are not disagreeing with you. But what if those like you who are now aware of this are launching some rockets of desire—

I am, big-time.

And what if, instead of having the conversation of what's wrong with the food, you're having conversations about what you want the results to be.

I'm doing that.

What if you become a light for the vibration of Well-Being? What if—with Source at your back and with the leverage that creates worlds—you shine a spotlight on that? What if that is the dominant vibration?

In the same way that when you were at your father's grave that day, and Source was flowing through you, and even though you had gone there to do something else to that grave that you ended up not doing . . . But because the vibration of Source is dominant, why not be the human form that focuses on the solution rather than the problem? And that is the only thing that has gone a little haywire with humans. You spend too much time talking about what you don't want, instead of articulating what you do want. So your frequencies and momentum are more about what you do not want.

But don't we have to be aware of what we don't want? I don't want to have my family eating genetically modified foods.

Of course. But listen, just in this conversation, to the amount of time you've spent on the topic of what you do not want as compared to the topic of what you do want—to what you could be doing about it.

I know and I am doing something about it.

Think about how they're not trucking in any food from other planets and that the seeds are all here. Wouldn't it be nice if in the modification of food, engineered food, there was a discovery of something that would be beneficial? And are you willing to accept that some of that has taken place, or could take place?

But you personally prevent yourself from experiencing the benefit of any of that when you push so hard against what you do not want. And really what it comes down to is the difference between living in a world where you are on lower-flying discs, fighting with each other, deciding which pile is the worst pile and which pile is a little bit better pile and no one really being in tune with Source, as compared to someone who sets all of that aside, who has the benefit of the desire that's born from that, who now turns to your Vortex, gets distracted from all of the issues that prevent you from resonance with Well-Being, and finds something like a little boy named Jessie to resonate with. And for the time that you are looking at that baby, you are in sync with all of the good things that you have been asking for.

The misunderstanding that humans have is they believe that they have to find the problem, get to the bottom of it, and wrestle it to the ground and kill it. And we want you to understand that there is no bottom to that. You are only adding vibrational momentum. And you can't win in that way. You cannot get to what you desire in that way.

Meanwhile, those who aren't all tied up in that, not paying any attention to that, can find a better way. Masses commonly fuss and fume and fight with one another, while a Steve Jobs or a Bill Gates finds a solution that revolutionizes the technology world. Everybody had the ability to do it. You only have to focus upon what you desire, instead of getting bogged down in the muck and mire of *what-is*.

You said it. You have to believe it before you see it.

It's a good book title.

It's the best. It's the best book title ever. It says everything. You have to find a way of believing what you want, because if you don't believe what you want, what you want cannot come.

Well, I have connected with the people at public television where I've done many specials, and I have agreed to begin to inform the entire planet, beginning with America and Canada, about—

We think that is wonderful. We just ask one thing. Get on your high-flying disc and then tell them what you know. Get the vibration of Source going with you. Talk about what can be, not about what can't be. Talk about where you're going, not about where you are. Talk about what's possible, not about the mess you're in. Get on the high-flying disc and let Source speak the words through you. You do it all the time. Just not when you talk about this.

Well, that pisses me off so much. And I know that being in that state of being upset is . . . You know, I've never really quite thought of it that way.

Moviemakers have discovered that more people go to the ornery movies, the dysfunctional movies, than the high-flying-disc movies. So if their goal is numbers and ratings, then they make a movie that appeals to where most people are. But that's not *who-you-are*. You've got to make a movie that appeals to God. [Playfully] We pulled out all the stops for that one.

Just for a second, can't you acknowledge that . . . you know, that it is companies owning seeds?

That *Law of Attraction* is broken? You want us to acknowledge that *Law of Attraction* is broken when it isn't? We will acknowledge that there's a momentum going, and we'll acknowledge the rage of the world and that the more people who are focused upon it the more momentum is added to it.

And we will also acknowledge that as more know what they don't want, then more will know what they do want, and there will be a tipping point. We just don't think you should suffer so long before the tipping point.

Well, I think what you just said will help the tipping point where we can indeed begin to focus on how we want our food supply to be, and how healthy we want our children to be.

Oh, when was the last time that you devoured some ripe piece of fruit right off the tree? Did you have to read the label to know it was good? Doesn't everything about you let you know the perfection of it when it's in alignment with *who-you-are?*

I live on Maui. And all of the fruits there don't even have seeds in them anymore. The papayas have all been genetically modified so you open it up and you used to think, *I'll take these seeds and I'll put them in the ground and I'll grow some papayas.* You're not allowed to do that anymore. You have to go to Monsanto to do that.

Oh, we have so much more to say to you.

I don't want to open a watermelon that doesn't have any seeds in it because it's been genetically modified.

Have all of them been genetically modified?

Ninety-nine percent on Maui have, yes.

Then pick the one that hasn't and revel in it. And say, "This feels best to me. This is what I support. This is what I promote." Because when you push against what you don't want, you practice that vibration of unwanted. And then *Law of Attraction* brings Monsanto to you to give you what you are vibrationally asking for.

It's not fair when it's my . . . This is something that really, really—

Well, if you were talking about things you don't care about, you wouldn't have launched these powerful rockets of desire. If you were talking about something that you don't care about, you wouldn't have just enlisted the Non-Physical Energy that creates worlds to support you. In other words, this conversation has catapulted this to a place that it never has been before. The Universe has expanded as a result of this conversation. You cannot find a solution if you don't poke around a little bit at the problem. Just don't get carried away in the poking around at the problem, because you cannot find a solution while you are poking at the problem. The problem and the solution are different vibrational frequencies.

The blame you feel, no matter how justified you are, does not lead you to the solution, you see. Have you ever had an argument with someone and you know you are right? You tell them what you think. Don't they just come on stronger and stronger and stronger and stronger? It is pouring gasoline on a fire.

149

Abraham's View
of the Political Arena

---•◦•---

It's kind of like what's happening in the political arena today with two sides just so determined that their side is correct. So there is not even any possibility of compromise.

Well, they've stopped thinking. And they cannot be feeling. But it's not all lost, because the electorate is feeling a desire for a functioning government.

And you—the people of the electorate—are in charge. But if you watch what the politicians are doing and you let them upset you, then you don't find your power, and so your desires are not realized.

We were talking with a woman on the telephone years ago, when Esther was still doing private consultations, who wasn't having any of this. She was annoyed with us. And since we were not making any headway with her, we said, "Let's play a game. We would like you to find three subjects, and let's just focus on them together."

She said, "Why?"

We said, "Because we want to distract you from your resistant thoughts. Because in the absence of resistance, many things you want will begin flowing to you."

"Well, like what?" she asked.

We said, "Like blue glass. Have you ever contemplated how many beautiful different textures and colors of blue glass there are?"

"No, I haven't, really, and I'm not really interested in that."

"Have you ever thought about butterflies, the variety of them, the longevity of them, the persistence of them, the beauty of them?"

"I don't really care about butterflies, either."

"Have you ever thought about feathers? Feathers are all around. Different kinds of feathers, benefiting all kinds of creatures." She hung up, annoyed with us.

Jerry and Esther were in La Jolla, California, that day, and so after the consultation they went down to George's to have lunch. Jerry had not heard the conversation. Esther was not really remembering it. As they were walking down the main street in La Jolla past La Valencia Hotel, Esther had such a strong urge to go inside a shop and so she dragged Jerry in. He did not want to go, but Esther was strong about it. So he followed her in, all the way to the back of the shop and on the back wall was the most amazing display of blue glass that either of them had ever seen. They didn't want blue glass. They didn't care about buying any blue glass. But nevertheless, there was blue glass.

So they left, without buying anything in the shop. They went to George's and had lunch, and then they walked down to the La Jolla cove, which in their opinion is the most beautiful place where the land meets the sea. They love that place.

As they were walking across the lawn on their way to the cliff, a flurry of butterflies, so intense they had to stop talking in order not to eat them, surrounded them.

Really?

Still Esther did not make the association with the telephone consultation. And then a little Asian boy who looked to be about three or four years old came running across the grass looking at Esther, holding something in his hand. He came directly to her and handed her a feather. And in that moment, it all came back to Esther. Then she realized that in less than two hours, the Universe had orchestrated a very clear, very clever path of least resistance to satisfy all three subjects that had been suggested with no resistance.

So it is our encouragement that you choose some things that you don't have a big wad of resistance about—not a cause, not a mission, not a life's purpose, not something that you're all wadded up about—and think about it. Just pick something easy and ponder it lightly in the morning when you wake up, and watch how clever the Universe is at helping you to rendezvous with it.

And if you do this enough, you will come to know that there is nothing outside your range, because when you tune to your true desire, meaning Source is with you in that desire, in the absence of resistance, all things are possible.

And all manner of things will take place. People will be amazed at what they see. "What are these politicians doing?" they will ask. "They're actually talking to each other. They do not usually talk to each other. They're actually beginning to seem reasonable. They're actually beginning to work together."

Wouldn't it be nice if a body of people, like those brilliant political people, with degrees and purpose, could come together and listen with reason, and tune in to the Source within them, not caring whose idea it is, or who gets the credit, but just reveling in the perfection of the idea?

This is the world that is possible for you, and it only takes a handful of you to focus in that way, you see. But as long as you are beating the drum of what's wrong with the politicians, you will add momentum to that, and you will defeat your own purpose. And you distract yourself from your true trajectory, and you feel bad in the process. And you blame the others for the way you feel.

You are powerful creators, you see. You're not facers of reality. You're creators of reality.

So even in the things that just seem most outrageous and most evil and most—

The more outrageous they are, the stronger your desire and the more Source is on it. You can't get there instantly we understand. But you've got to care enough about how you feel that you start practicing yourself into the vicinity until your sense of wor-thiness descends consistently upon you and you are willing to then take on the big subjects and focus on the big solutions.

Then anger doesn't motivate you to that?

Motivation is a whole different thing than in-spiration. Motivation is just unpleasant. Inspiration always feels good. It's a first step; we don't deny that. Just don't stay so long in that first step. Makes you tired and grouchy and cynical and then you become a politician.

Dyer-Abraham Event Close

───────── ● ● ● ─────────

We have enjoyed this interaction more than words can ever explain.

As have I.

It is delicious to take thought beyond. There is great love here for you. [Addressing the audience] And for you.

Thank you.

We are complete.

Esther: Thank you, Hay House. Thank all of you. This was a great day.

Wayne: Thank you. Got those tinglies. I don't know what they are, but they're tinglies. Love you. Good night. Thank you for coming.

ABOUT THE AUTHORS

Dr. Wayne W. Dyer is an internationally renowned author and speaker in the field of self-development. He's the author of more than 40 books, has created many audio programs and videos, and has appeared on thousands of television and radio shows. His books *Manifest Your Destiny, Wisdom of the Ages, There's a Spiritual Solution to Every Problem,* and the *New York Times* bestsellers *10 Secrets for Success and Inner Peace, The Power of Intention, Inspiration, Change Your Thoughts—Change Your Life, Excuses Begone!, Wishes Fulfilled,* and *I Can See Clearly Now* have all been featured as National Public Television specials.

Wayne holds a doctorate in educational counseling from Wayne State University and was an associate professor at St. John's University in New York.

Website: www.DrWayneDyer.com

#1 *New York Times* best-selling authors **Esther** and **Jerry Hicks** have been producing the Leading Edge Abraham-Hicks teachings since 1986. In November 2011, Jerry made his transition into Non-Physical, and now Esther continues to conduct the Abraham seminars with the help of her physical friends and co-workers and, of course, with the Non-Physical help of Abraham and Jerry.

Their internationally acclaimed website is: www .abraham-hicks.com.

HAY HOUSE TITLES OF RELATED INTEREST

YOU CAN HEAL YOUR LIFE, the movie,
starring Louise Hay & Friends
(available as a 1-DVD program
and an expanded 2-DVD set)
Watch the trailer at: www.LouiseHayMovie.com

∽

ADVENTURES OF THE SOUL: Journeys Through the
Physical and Spiritual Dimensions, by James Van Praagh

CHUANG TSU: Inner Chapters, translated
by Gia-fu Feng and Jane English

CONVERSATIONS WITH HISTORY:
Inspiration, Reflections, and Advice from History-Makers
and Celebrities on the Other Side, by Susan Lander

THE TOP TEN THINGS DEAD PEOPLE
WANT TO TELL YOU, by Mike Dooley

YOU CAN CREATE AN EXCEPTIONAL LIFE,
by Louise Hay and Cheryl Richardson

All of the above are available at your local bookstore,
or may be ordered by contacting Hay House (see next page).

∽

We hope you enjoyed this Hay House book. If you'd like to receive our online catalog featuring additional information on Hay House books and products, or if you'd like to find out more about the Hay Foundation, please contact:

Hay House, Inc., P.O. Box 5100, Carlsbad, CA 92018-5100
(760) 431-7695 or (800) 654-5126
(760) 431-6948 (fax) or (800) 650-5115 (fax)
www.hayhouse.com® • www.hayfoundation.org

∽

Published and distributed in Australia by: Hay House
Australia Pty. Ltd., 18/36 Ralph St., Alexandria NSW 2015
Phone: 612-9669-4299 • *Fax:* 612-9669-4144
www.hayhouse.com.au

Published and distributed in the United Kingdom by:
Hay House UK, Ltd., Astley House, 33 Notting Hill Gate,
London W11 3JQ • *Phone:* 44-20-3675-2450
Fax: 44-20-3675-2451 • www.hayhouse.co.uk

Published and distributed in the Republic of South Africa by:
Hay House SA (Pty), Ltd., P.O. Box 990, Witkoppen 2068
Phone/Fax: 27-11-467-8904 • www.hayhouse.co.za

Published in India by: Hay House Publishers India, Muskaan
Complex, Plot No. 3, B-2, Vasant Kunj, New Delhi 110 070
Phone: 91-11-4176-1620 • *Fax:* 91-11-4176-1630
www.hayhouse.co.in

Distributed in Canada by: Raincoast Books, 2440 Viking Way,
Richmond, B.C. V6V 1N2 • *Phone:* 1-800-663-5714
Fax: 1-800-565-3770 • www.raincoast.com

◡

Take Your Soul on a Vacation

Visit www.HealYourLife.com® to regroup, recharge,
and reconnect with your own magnificence.
Featuring blogs, mind-body-spirit news, and life-changing
wisdom from Louise Hay and friends.

Visit www.HealYourLife.com today!

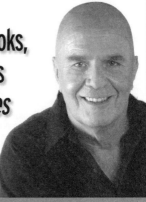

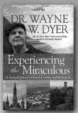